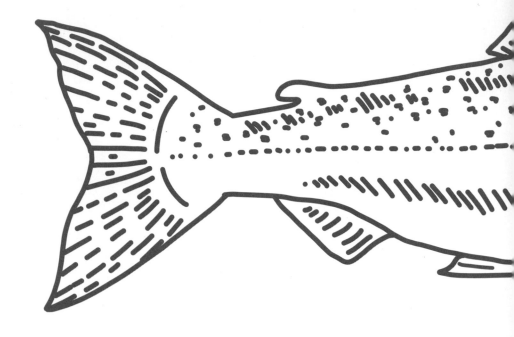

EMMA TEAL LAUKITIS —— CLAIRE NEATON

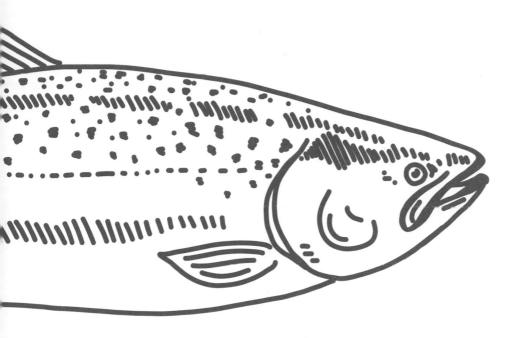

The Salmon Sisters

Feasting, Fishing, and Living in Alaska

SASQUATCH BOOKS

SEATTLE

Printed in China

SASQUATCH BOOKS with colophon is a registered trademark
of Penguin Random House LLC

24 23 22 21 20   9 8 7 6 5 4 3 2 1

Editor: Gary Luke
Illustrator: Emma Teal Laukitis

Photographs: Brian Grobleski except for pages 4-5, 12-13, 24, 92-93, 200,
208 by Sashwa Burrous; 1, 8, 147 by Camrin Dengel; 10, 11, 14, 25, 27, 119,
135, 199, 202 by Scott Dickerson; 20 and back endpaper author photo by Dawn
Heumann; 49 by Xesai/istockphoto.com; 109 by blueenayim/istockphoto.com;
front endpaper photo by temmuzcan/istockphoto.com

Library of Congress Cataloging-in-Publication Data

Names: Laukitis, Emma Teal, author. | Neaton, Claire, author.
Title: The salmon sisters : feasting, fishing, and living in Alaska / Emma
    Teal Laukitis, Claire Neaton.
Description: Seattle : Sasquatch Books, 2020. | Includes bibliographical
    references and index. | Summary: "Feasting, fishing, and living in
    Alaska. A cookbook with 50 recipes"-- Provided by publisher.
Identifiers: LCCN 2019022793 (print) | LCCN 2019022794 (ebook) | ISBN
    9781632172259 (hardcover) | ISBN 9781632172266 (ebook)
Subjects: LCSH: Cooking (Salmon)--Alaska. | Cooking--Alaska. | LCGFT:
    Cookbooks.
Classification: LCC TX748.S24 L38 2020 (print) | LCC TX748.S24 (ebook) |
    DDC 641.6/92--dc23
LC record available at https://lccn.loc.gov/2019022793
LC ebook record available at https://lccn.loc.gov/2019022794

ISBN: 978-1-63217-225-9

Sasquatch Books
1904 Third Avenue, Suite 710
Seattle, WA 98101
SasquatchBooks.com

For Shelly,
our salmon mom

Contents

Welcome to Alaska

INSIDE THIS BOOK

Living by the sea has inspired the way our family works, eats, and lives. Good food is all around us—at low tide, under rocks, deep in the ocean, swimming up rivers. It can grow on the beach, in garden beds, on the tundra, or in the forest. Good food can be fresh and simple, like salmon pulled straight from the sea that is seasoned with a sprinkle of salt and cooked over a driftwood fire on the shore. Good food can also be creative—unlikely ingredients combined in a single pot on a boat's small galley stovetop. It can be resourceful, like a fresh batch of yogurt started with a spoonful from an old one. It can follow tradition—a family's smoked salmon recipe or sourdough starter passed down through generations. Good food is eaten with recognition of the natural bounty that has provided its nourishment.

We have made this book to share our fishing family's love for cooking and to honor Alaska's wild bounty with the stories, recipes, and artwork in the pages that follow. From memories of our mom smoking salmon on our homestead to learning how to cook at sea, we offer a glimpse into our unique upbringing and way of life as fishermen. We hope it makes our readers feel more connected to the people working hard to bring seafood to their tables, more aware of the edible wild plants and ocean creatures around them, and inspired to make some of our favorite simple and flavorful recipes.

OUR FISHING FAMILY'S RECIPES

Straight from the big blue three-ring binder our mom has kept on the kitchen shelf since we were kids, the recipes in this book were collected from villagers and fishermen in the Aleutian Islands, grandparents, and friends who have become our Alaska family. The recipes focus on ingredients abundant in Alaska—fresh seafood, garden-grown vegetables, and edible wild plants and berries—that can be enjoyed by home cooks everywhere.

There are no supermarkets at sea, so when our family cooks on the boat, we often start with our freshest, most exciting ingredient (a rockfish, or maybe a bucket of wild blueberries picked on the shore) and then let creativity take over. Most of these recipes allow for an improvisational cooking style: they have simple instructions, often flexible ingredients, and tasty results. They are suitable for cooking in small spaces like a boat's galley, or in a fully stocked kitchen with counter space to spare. Our family has been making these dishes for many years; the recipes have given us a strong understanding of how good food can be prepared and eaten. We hope these recipes encourage confidence in you too, especially with seafood. We invite you to write in the margins of the following pages and make the recipes your own, because going off the chart sometimes allows for the greatest discoveries.

WILD ALASKA SEAFOOD: NOW AND FOREVER

The ocean has provided our family with nourishment and meaningful work. Our days revolve around the tides, the fish, and the weather in a fluid rhythm of the seasons. We spend our days working on Alaska's

North Pacific Ocean—bringing health, joy, and a story to the people who enjoy our wild catch.

Alaska's fisheries are anchored in strict conservation practices, to ensure that the ocean ecosystem continues to thrive and that delicious wild-caught seafood will be enjoyed for generations to come. Alaska's government is one of few in the world that is truly dedicated to sustainability. This commitment dates back to statehood in 1959, when citizens wrote protections for the responsible management of fisheries into Alaska's constitution. The secret to Alaska's success lies in two basic principles: First, fishermen, scientists, and government agree on fishing practices that take care not to harm fish, marine plants and animals, or the environment. Second, fish populations are managed for sustainability, assuring there are enough left to replenish the natural population. Alaska is one of the last places on earth where people still depend on wild salmon to thrive and return each year.

We're proud that the role our family plays in the delicate balance of harvesting wild seafood from the ocean is future-thinking, and that each year our pristine ocean continues to run wild with marine life. The fish we harvest are much more than a commodity to catch and sell; they are a source of nourishment, tradition, and connection to the wild places where we live and work. Reverence for fish in Alaska can be seen in Native arts dating back centuries, as well as in the fishing practices of the thousands of families who today make their living off the sea. In fact, fishing and seafood processing employ more people than any other industry in Alaska.

Being responsible stewards of the ocean means that our family will be able to continue fishing for decades to come. It also means that Alaska's fishing communities can continue to bring the sea to tables around the world. The physical strength, mental grit, and sacrifice that goes into working on the water makes fishing a unique and challenging occupation, but it also brings many joys—a rich heritage, freedom, camaraderie, ingenuity, and enterprise. This book offers readers a glimpse both at an occupation that is a way of life for many and also at the people whose lives respond to the tides.

MADE OF SALMON

Sometimes it seems we are made of salmon, since it's the food most often shared around our family's table and the fish we harvest each summer.

We've spent every summer of our lives following the life cycle of salmon. As kids, we spent our days catching sockeye in our mom's net, hauling them up the beach to the fish-cleaning table in the tall beach grass and then filleting, stripping, and brining them for our family's smokehouse. Our salmon hung to dry in the gusty Aleutian wind, slowly seasoned with cottonwood smoke from driftwood logs washed up in front of our homestead as well as salt from the sea. Smoked salmon was our family's most valuable asset. We brought it to friends when we visited the village, mailed it to our relatives in the Lower 48, served it when special guests sat around our kitchen table, and received it in care packages from our parents when we were away at college.

We have carried our family's tradition of sharing wild seafood into our business, Salmon Sisters. We founded our Give Fish Project in 2016 to give back to the community that has supported us over the years. Eating wild Alaska seafood makes us feel healthy, happy, and strong, which is something we want to share with as many people as possible. One percent of our sales is set aside to purchase wild Alaska seafood, which we give to the Food Bank of Alaska—supporting both seafood harvesters and those in need of nutrient-rich seafood. One in seven people and one in five children struggle with hunger in Alaska, and we are grateful for the opportunity to play a part in tackling food insecurity by sharing the bounty of our local ocean.

Our small company is just one way we thank the ocean for all it has given us. We work hard to celebrate the beautiful creatures living beneath the waves, and the North Pacific's thriving fisheries with our artwork, clothing, and design.

OUR SALMON FAMILY

The two of us have always worked together—whether we were digging up potatoes from our mom's garden or baiting halibut hooks on a fishing trip with our dad. Only a year apart in age, we grew up on a remote homestead a boat ride away from any other kids our age, so we learned to tackle the world side by side from the very beginning. We are now business partners and run our company, Salmon Sisters, while we continue to commercial fish with our family.

Education and experience have helped shape the direction of our work; we grew up surrounded by creativity, self-sufficiency, respect for wild places, and an understanding of our interdependence within the marine ecosystem. Our parents, like many Alaska fishermen, own and operate their own businesses, and they have inspired us to invest in our own individual skills and opportunities and to take risks for our passions.

We both left Alaska for college on the East Coast and quickly realized how unique our childhood had been. It was difficult to describe our seasonal work as fishermen to peers and professors, the remoteness of our home in the Aleutian Islands, and our insistence on returning each summer to fish instead of applying for career-building internships. College tuitions were paid with the money we made from summer fishing jobs. Plus, we always craved the physical work and joy of being outside after long winters of lectures, papers, and hours in the library.

Claire studied business and marketing at the University of Vermont, and Emma studied English and studio art at Williams College in Massachusetts before earning her master's degree in design at the University of Washington. Our hard and soft skills complement each other's, and our shared experiences at sea have helped us "weather the storm" of owning a small business together.

Our dad, Buck, spends his days trying to think like a fish: he runs the FV (fishing vessel) *Stanley K* in Prince William Sound and out to the Bering Sea, following salmon and halibut in a shared seasonal migration. Our family's other boats, the FV *Oracle* and FV *Halcyon*, operate as tenders during the summer and participate in pot cod fisheries in the

Bering Sea, Aleutian Islands, and western Gulf of Alaska, as well as the westward halibut grounds year-round. In the winters, our dad does his part to ensure that fisheries policies help fishermen keep their vessels working and profitable and that the future of coastal communities is not sacrificed in the process.

Our mom, Shelly—much like Steve Zissou's wife, Eleanor, in *The Life Aquatic*—is known to be the brains behind the operation. She has provided onshore support for many years while her husband and daughters spent the summers fishing. She climbs aboard the boats for a few weeks each summer, and we always look forward to her company. Incredible meals suddenly spring from the galley, and an endless flow of fresh coffee fills our cups. Our boat freezer is quickly packed with blueberries she picks onshore, shrimp she catches in our pots, and king salmon she saves for the winter. It is thanks to Mom that the recipes in this book exist.

Our husbands are fishermen as well. Though neither of them grew up in Alaska, they have been shaped by its ocean much as we have. Peter and Jacob work year-round on the water—in the winter they catch Pacific cod in the Bering Sea and western Gulf of Alaska, and in the summer they fish and tender for salmon, with a few months of black cod and halibut fishing in between.

Our family is close-knit. With equal parts ambition and thoughtfulness, we have managed to build a dynamic fishing business in which we are all participants. Our family no longer returns to the homestead at Stonewall Place, as we began spending more time on the boat fishing and less on land during the summers. Mom kept Stonewall running while we were fishing with Papa through college, but she had spent enough years keeping company alone with brown bears. Still, a day doesn't go by that we don't think about our wonderful and challenging life there. Our nostalgia for our home fills this book.

Sometimes it seems our work is endless—there are always nets to build, boats to paint, fish to catch, accounting to settle, crew to hire, fishing gear to take on and off the boat, policy to attend to, weather forecasts to watch, and on top of everything, people to feed. This book exists because, despite the work at hand, our family has always made time for good food. We remove our gloves, wash the fish scales from our faces, and sit down to enjoy our bounty together.

From the Sea

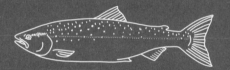

Cooking on the Boat

Our parents started their careers as fishermen in their early twenties, both transplants from the Lower 48. Papa got a job on a fishing boat sailing north from Seattle, and Mom answered an ad in a local newspaper for a job at a lodge in Glacier Bay National Park. After a few seasons in southeast Alaska, they moved west to the Aleutian Islands, where fishing opportunity was vast, and a small homestead on the tip of the Alaska Peninsula became their home. They learned to setnet for salmon in Ikatan Bay, an abandoned cannery village near False Pass and just a few miles away from our homestead by skiff. They seined for herring in the spring Togiak fishery and longlined for halibut near Dutch Harbor and King Cove in the fall. Eventually they bought a forty-two-foot gillnet boat named the FV *Lucky Dove*, which became our family's boat and seasonal home for most of our childhood.

Papa spent his summers fishing around Unimak Island while Mom ran the homestead—fending off hungry brown bears and looking after the garden, chickens, and the two of us until we were old enough to join our dad on the water. On the boat we helped Papa pick salmon from the gill net, lift levers that ran the hydraulics, and spot jumping fish from the flying bridge. We brought stacks of books borrowed from the small village library to read at the galley table and studied the names of salmon species, seabirds, neighboring volcanoes, and the boats in our fleet. We wrote letters to our friends who spent their summers fishing too, many of them with their families in other remote parts of the state. It might take a month for mail to pass between us, so sometimes we just slipped our messages into empty bottles and threw them to the waves, hoping the sea might deliver them more quickly than boats or planes would. But our first real job, before we were big or strong enough to run the back deck or clean halibut, was to cook.

We learned how to grind coffee beans and to always keep the coffee pot full. We made bread and muffins and cookies in the finicky propane oven on the *Lucky Dove*, and prepared the fresh fish we caught in our net. We took turns cooking bacon and eggs and blueberry

pancakes on the stovetop in the mornings. It was nice to stay inside where it was warm, but when the seas were rough, we both preferred to be out in the fresh air instead of in the galley. Bad weather taught us tricks for holding pots of boiling water in place, keeping bowls of soup upright, and bungee-cording the coffee pot to the wall. Being seasick is one of the worst feelings, but coming inside after a long day of work to a good meal is one of the best, so we always tried to look out at the horizon while we cooked and endure the queasiness for as long as it took to make one for the crew.

Our dad, perhaps because he has grown used to the delicious meals flowing from our mom's kitchen, considers good food to be one of the most important parts of life. He has always given mealtimes at sea a special importance. While scouting for jumping salmon through his binoculars or jotting notes into his logbook or answering calls on the radio, he would call out to whoever might hear: "What about some beer-battered halibut?" or "I was thinking about cookies." After exchanging a sideways sisterly look, we got to work.

Every time we left the homestead, we geared up with bundles of fresh greens and radishes and cherry tomatoes and carrots and potatoes from the garden. After a few weeks at sea, our vegetable supply ran low, and we resorted to a regular diet of fresh salmon with rice, seaweed, sesame seeds, and soy sauce—a staple meal for our family that somehow we've never grown tired of. Catching fish so fresh and

sharing it around a tiny galley table after a long day of work might have something to do with it.

On days when fishing was closed and we were far from home, we anchored up somewhere protected from the wind and waves with other fishermen in our fleet, our boats rafted together for the night. Captains and crew crowded into one boat's cabin, telling stories until the midnight sun slept, weaving comedy and tragedy into their memories. Young deckhands listened intently, witness to both the exuberance and melancholy of their captains' experiences at sea, and learning to spin tales of their own. We often made meals together on these nights, tossing tortillas across the deck, peeling potato skins into the sea, and swapping hot sauces and pots and pans in a dance between our rafted boats.

Cooking is a pastime and a way to express ourselves creatively during a fishing season without phone service or internet or news aside from the constant chatter on the radio. With limited ingredients and without the ability to quickly google a recipe, it's sometimes hard to envision a meal. But when we let ourselves enjoy the challenge of using ingredients in a nontypical way, wonderful things can happen. Serving up a delicious dish on the boat means we can raise spirits when weather is bad or fishing is slow. Fishing days are long and intense, and we are often working twenty hours straight with only a few hours to sleep. A pan of brownies or a pot of halibut chowder might make the difference between a forgettable day and a memorable one.

It is difficult to get fresh vegetables on the boat, especially when we're at sea for weeks at a time, but healthy meals are still possible. Some summers we bring plants on the boat and they grow happily in the window or on the top deck. Potatoes, onions, cabbage, garlic, and ginger keep well for a long time in a cool, dry place on the boat, and more perishable vegetables can be preserved by canning or pickling to be enjoyed for many months. Plus, there is nothing more nutritious than fish fresh from the ocean. We enjoy eating as many parts of the fish as we can all summer long—fried salmon skin makes for a delicious crunchy snack, and cod tongues taste like scallops when cooked in butter. Fish bones and tails make good stock for soups, and salted salmon roe is a delicacy on rice or crackers.

Something we love about living and eating on the boat is the joy that comes from a juicy orange, a decadent chocolate bar, or a bowl of ice cream from a tender's freezer. One time we gave a bunch of cilantro to another crew who hadn't been to town in over a month, and one of them cried actual tears of joy. These moments that can be taken for granted when we're on land are absolutely savored at sea—the simple pleasure of eating good food.

Commercial Fishing Methods in Alaska

SALMON

GILL NET

Most of the boats fishing for salmon in Alaska use gill nets. They are set out like a wall in the water, either drifting in the ocean or set with anchors. The fish swim into the net until their heads become entangled, which prevents them from escaping. Most gillnetters are small one- and two-person boats between thirty-two and forty-two feet long. Gill net fishermen target sockeye (red) salmon.

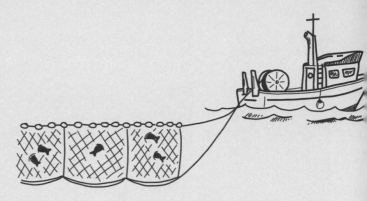

PURSE SEINE

Large numbers of salmon are caught with seines in southeastern, central, and western Alaska. A purse seine is a net that is set in a circular shape around schools of fish and then drawn closed at the bottom to be hauled aboard. Purse seiners are generally larger than gillnetters, but are limited to fifty-eight feet by Alaska law. Seine fishermen target pink salmon.

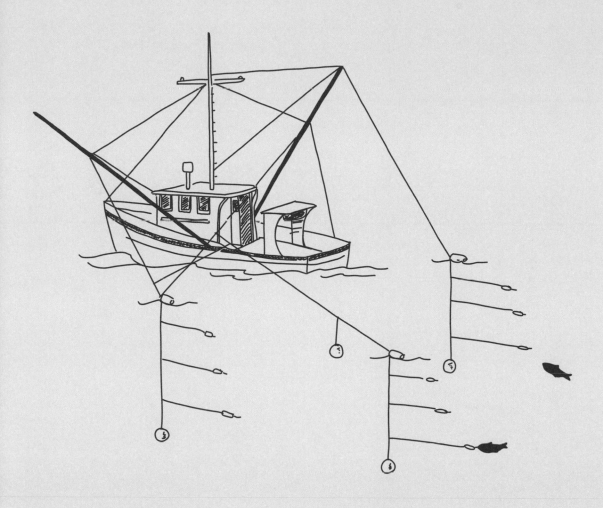

TROLL

Trollers are small fishing vessels operated by one or two people who fish with baited hooks and lines. The volume of troll-caught fish is less than 10 percent of the total Alaska catch of all salmon species because they come aboard one at a time. However, what trollers lack in quantity, they make up for in quality. Each troll-caught fish is handled individually and carefully, making them the most valuable, pound for pound, of all the salmon caught in Alaska.

WHITEFISH

LONGLINE

Longline gear is used to harvest halibut, black cod, and Pacific cod. Some longliners catch, ice, and hold their catch for several days before delivering them to shore; others are larger vessels that catch, process, and freeze their catch at sea. Longline gear is composed of groundline, buoy lines that attach to heavy anchors on one end and buoys on the other, and gangions, which are short pieces of line with baited circle hooks on the end. Longlines are set along the seabed, with hooks spaced several yards apart. Longline hooks are retrieved one at a time as the longline is pulled aboard by the boat's hydraulics, and the fish are unhooked individually. Nontarget fish species are released and returned alive to the sea without bringing them on board.

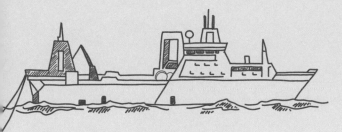

TRAWL

A trawl is a large bag-shaped net that is towed behind a fishing vessel to catch fish in its path. Trawlers (not to be confused with trollers) are some of the largest vessels fishing in Alaska, typically ranging from seventy to over two hundred feet in length. The doors of the net are built and rigged to keep the mouth of the trawl open as it moves through the water, with floats on the upper opening and weights on the lower opening.

Trawlers use electronic-sounding to locate fish underwater and identify their species. Pollock are caught using midwater trawls that avoid contact with the bottom of the ocean, minimizing damage to the benthic habitat and incidental catch of nontarget species. Pacific cod and sole are caught with bottom trawls, which are allowed only in certain areas and have strictly enforced bycatch limits.

POTS

Pots are normally used to harvest black cod, Pacific cod, and crab. Pots are constructed of large steel frames covered in net mesh. The baited pots are lowered to the sea-floor where fish or crab enter the traps through tunnels with one-way doors to prevent escape. Later the pots are retrieved and sorted on deck; nontarget species are returned alive to the sea.

SHELLFISH

CLAMS:
Hard-shell clams like littlenecks and razors are harvested in the cold water of the Cook Inlet and Kachemak Bay regions. They are dug using hand shovels and clam guns.

CRAB:
Dungeness, king, and snow crab are harvested by crabbing, a fishing method utilizing steel pots or traps baited with cut fish. Buoys mark the location of each pot on the ocean floor and the name of its owner. After soaking for several hours to several days, depending on the weather and tides, the pots are hauled in, quickly emptied into the hold, rebaited, and returned to the ocean floor.

GEODUCKS, SEA URCHINS, AND SEA CUCUMBERS:
Geoducks, sea urchins, and sea cucumbers are generally harvested in the cold clean water of southeast Alaska by individual divers who gather these species from the seafloor by hand.

SCALLOPS:
Alaska scallops are harvested with dredges that collect scallops on the ocean floor. The dredges are deployed and towed slowly for fifty to sixty minutes, retrieved, and then scallops are sorted on deck, hand-shucked, flash-frozen, and packaged onboard, ensuring quality texture and taste.

SHRIMP:
Harvested from the Aleutian Islands to southeast Alaska, pink shrimp are caught with bottom trawls and beam trawls. Spot shrimp, Alaska's largest and most valued shrimp species, are caught with pots in generally steep, rough ocean floor terrain.

The Catch in the Kitchen

SALMON

Salmon has a rich and distinct flavor that can be enjoyed in any favorite dish. There are many ways to prepare fresh or frozen salmon, but the basic rule is to cook it for 10 minutes per inch of thickness. Whatever you do, don't overcook it.

To grill: Place salmon steaks or fillets on a medium-high heat, well-greased grill. Grill for 10 minutes per inch, brushing often with butter, oil, or marinade. With skin on, fish does not need to be flipped. Flip once if skinless. Test doneness by flaking the fish with a fork at its thickest part.

To bake: Place whole salmon (stuffed with herbs, if desired) in a well-greased baking pan. Brush the fish with oil or melted butter and bake at 400 degrees F for 10 minutes per inch. (Measure the fish at the thickest part; if it's stuffed, include the stuffing in the measurement.) It is done cooking when the fish flakes when tested with a fork at its thickest part. Do not flip during baking.

To broil: Place salmon steaks or fillets on a well-greased baking pan. Brush with oil, melted butter, or marinade. Broil about 4 inches from the broiler for 10 minutes per inch, flipping the salmon after 5 minutes and brushing again with oil, butter, or marinade. Test doneness by flaking the fish with a fork at its thickest part.

To sauté: In a large skillet over medium heat, heat ½ inch of oil or butter. Do not allow it to smoke. Sauté salmon steaks or fillets until golden brown on one side, then flip and brown on the other side. Cook for 10 minutes total per inch. Test doneness by flaking the fish with a fork at its thickest part.

PACIFIC SALMON

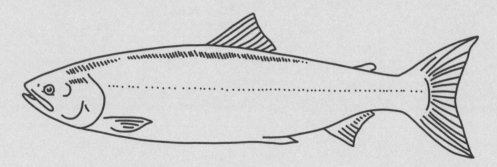

CHUM (KETA)

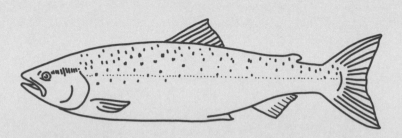

PINK (HUMPY)

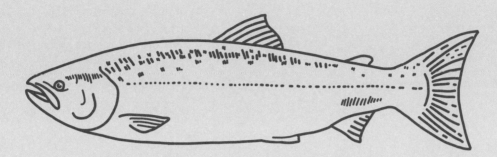

SILVER (COHO)

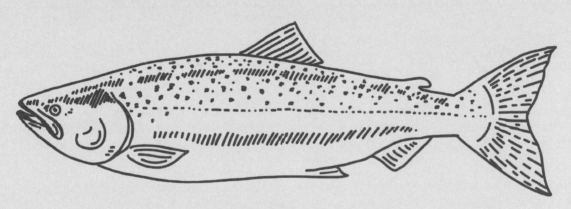

KING (CHINOOK)

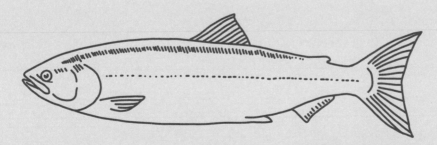

RED (SOCKEYE)

To poach: Place salmon steaks or fillets in a large Dutch oven and layer with 2 slices lemon, 2 slices onion, 1 sprig rosemary, several peppercorns. Cover with boiling salted water. Bring to a boil. Cover, reduce the heat to a simmer, and cook for 10 minutes per inch. Test doneness by flaking the fish with a fork at its thickest part.

SILVER
With its delicate texture, orange flesh, and light flavor, silver is a favorite for grilling. Also known as coho.

Season: Available fresh mid-June through late October and frozen year-round

Harvest Method: Trolling, gillnetting, purse seining

Size and Specs: Second largest of the five Alaska salmon species. Their average weight is about twelve pounds. Sold as whole, steaks, or fillets.

Preparation Suggestions: We like it best cooked into salmon cakes or grilled with minced garlic and a squeeze of lemon.

CHUM
Chum has a mild flavor and pink flesh with lower oil content. It's a versatile option for grilling, smoking, or adding to your favorite dish. Also known as keta.

Season: Available fresh June through September and frozen year-round

Harvest Method: Gillnetting, purse seining

Size and Specs: Average weight is eight pounds. Sold as whole, steaks, and fillets.

Preparation Suggestions: This is a fish very good for smoking, grilling, pickling, or adding to a favorite creamy chowder or ginger-soy stir fry. It's best prepared with lower cooking temperatures due to keta's low oil content. Chum salmon roe is considered a delicacy.

KING
Prized for its high oil content, firm texture, and succulent flesh; also known as Chinook.

Season: Available fresh or frozen year-round

Harvest Method: Trolling, gillnetting, purse seining

Size and Specs: Largest of the five Alaska salmon species. Average weight is twenty pounds. Sold as whole, steaks, or fillets.

Preparation Suggestions: The king's high oil content makes it perfect for grilling, broiling, poaching, or smoking. Its succulent flavor doesn't need much in the way of marinades or spices, but a dash of pepper and flaky sea salt with a few slices of lemon goes a long way.

PINK
Pink salmon has a mild, delicate flavor and pink flesh great for grilling or topping with a favorite sauce. An economical choice for a variety of recipes. Also known as humpys because of their arched backs.

Season: Available fresh mid-June through September and frozen year-round

Harvest Method: Purse seining, gillnetting, trolling

Size and Specs: Pinks are the smallest and most abundant of the five Alaska salmon species. Average weight is two to three pounds. Commonly available in convenient shelf-stable cans.

Preparation Suggestions: Pink salmon's light flavor makes it the perfect protein for dishes with additional spices or sauces. We love using pinks to make fish tacos with fresh salsa or salmon cakes with garlic aioli.

RED

With its firm texture, rich taste, and distinctive deep-red flesh, the red is one of the most flavorful salmon in the sea. It retains its color throughout the cooking process. Also known as sockeye.

Season: Available fresh May through September and frozen year-round

Harvest Method: Gillnetting, purse seining

Size and Specs: The second most abundant of Alaska's salmon species. Their weight is typically around six pounds. Sold as whole, steaks, or fillets and available as shelf-stable product forms like cans or pouches.

Preparation Suggestions: Red salmon is great for grilling, broiling, sautéing, poaching, or smoking. The red's natural flavor, color, and firmness goes a long way—it's perfect for making poke and lox. Our favorite everyday fish.

WHITEFISH

Naturally lean, with delicate, mild flavor and firm snow-white flesh, whitefish—including halibut, cod, and rockfish—are easy to cook and endlessly versatile.

There are many ways to prepare whitefish. The general rule is to cook it for 10 minutes per inch of thickness, measuring the fish at its thickest part.

To grill: Place steaks or fillets on a medium-heat, well-greased grill. Grill for 10 minutes per inch, flipping the fish once and brushing often with butter, oil, or marinade and finishing with a sprinkle of salt and pepper, herbs, or other seasoning. Test doneness by flaking the fish with a fork at its thickest part.

To bake: Place whole fish or steaks in a well-greased baking dish. Season with salt, pepper, and herbs. If desired, sprinkle with chopped vegetables. Sprinkle a mixture of lemon juice and butter over the top and bake at 400 degrees F for 10 minutes per inch. Test doneness by flaking the fish with a fork at its thickest part.

To broil: Season fillets or steaks with salt, pepper, and herbs, or marinate in any favorite sauce for about 1 hour. Broil about 4 inches from the broiler for 10 minutes per inch, brushing again with oil, butter, or marinade every 5 minutes. Test doneness by flaking the fish with a fork at its thickest part.

To sauté: Season fish with salt, pepper, and herbs. In a large skillet, heat ¼ inch of oil or butter. Do not allow it to smoke. Sauté fish steaks or fillets until golden brown on one side, then flip and brown on the other side. Cook for 10 minutes total per inch.

To poach: Place fish steaks or fillets in a large Dutch oven and layer with 2 slices lemon, 2 slices onion, 4 sprigs parsley, pepper, and salt. Cover with boiling salted water. Bring to a boil. Cover, reduce the heat to a simmer, and cook for 10 minutes per inch. Test doneness by flaking the fish with a fork at its thickest part.

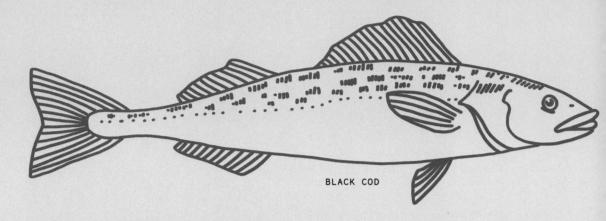

BLACK COD

WHITEFISH

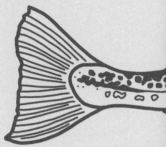

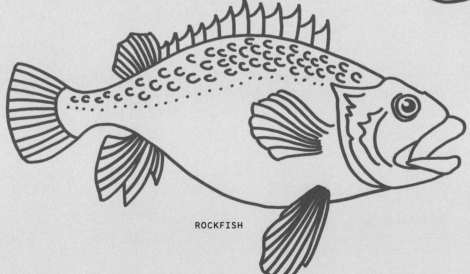

ROCKFISH

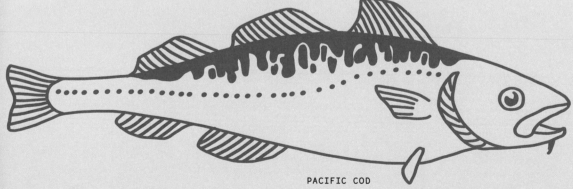

HALIBUT

POLLOCK

PACIFIC COD

To simmer: For stews and chowders, add fish chunks or cubes during the final 5 to 10 minutes of cooking. After the fish is added, do not overstir the stew.

To deep-fry: Cut fish into bite-size pieces and dip in batter and/or seasoned crumbs. Deep-fry at 375 degrees F for 2 or 3 minutes, or until the fish is golden brown and flakes easily when tested with a fork. Flip once during frying; drain on paper towels before serving.

BLACK COD

Prized for its rich, buttery, melt-in-your-mouth flavor and velvety texture. Also known as sablefish.

Season: Available fresh March through mid-November and frozen year-round

Harvest Method: Trawling, long-lining, pot fishing

Size and Specs: Alaska has the world's largest black cod population. Weighs an average of five to ten pounds. Sold fresh and frozen in fillet form.

Preparation Suggestions: Black cod's oil content makes it perfect for grilling, poaching, or smoking. It is especially delicious prepared with a miso-soy-ginger glaze.

HALIBUT

Its firm flake and delicate flavor have given Alaska halibut its reputation as the world's premium whitefish.

Season: Available fresh March through November and frozen year-round

Harvest Method: Long-lining

Size and Specs: Average weight is twenty-four to fifty pounds, though they can grow up to a gigantic four-hundred pounds. Generally marketed in fillet or steak forms. Roasts are also available, as are halibut cheeks, a delicacy to many.

Preparation Suggestions: Halibut maintains its firmness throughout cooking and is suitable for all types of preparation methods, but it's especially great for grilling, poaching, deep-frying, or adding to chowder or stews. Known as the "steak of seafood." We love grilling halibut with garlic mayonnaise, lemon slices, and fresh dill.

PACIFIC COD

Pacific cod has flesh that is firm and moist with a distinctive large flake and a delicately sweet flavor.

Season: Sometimes available fresh November through March and frozen year-round

Harvest Method: Trawling, long-lining, pot fishing, jig fishing

Size and Specs: Related to both Alaska pollock and Atlantic cod. Weighs an average of five to ten pounds. Commonly sold as skinless, boneless fillets or portions.

Preparation Suggestions: Pacific cod's firm texture makes it a great choice for most cooking methods. It can be poached, sautéed, flaked into a chowder or stew, or deep-fried for fish and chips or crunchy tacos. Delicious complemented by favorite marinades or sauces like garlic butter or aioli.

POLLOCK

Pollock's lean, snow-white flesh offers a flaky texture and mild taste that is incredibly versatile in the kitchen.

Season: Available frozen year-round (pollock is flash-frozen onboard immediately after it is caught)

Harvest Method: Trawling

Size and Specs: Alaska pollock is the largest fishery by volume in the United States and the second-largest in the world. Pollock is related to cod and shares many of the same attributes. Average weight is one and a half to two pounds.

Preparation Suggestions: Often available for purchase prepared and frozen in the form of fish sticks or burgers, it can be warmed and enjoyed in a wide variety of meals. To warm, just heat the fish as the packaging directs. Serve with a favorite dipping sauce like tartar sauce or sweet and spicy chili sauce.

ROCKFISH

Rockfish has deliciously moist and slightly sweet flesh with a large, firm flake. It's excellent in fish tacos or soup and pairs well with favorite rubs or sauces.

Season: Available fresh January through November and frozen year-round

Harvest Method: Trawling, long-lining, jig fishing

Size and Specs: Alaska is home to many species of rockfish, including northern, dusky, canary, widow, shortraker, rougheye, thornyhead, and Pacific ocean perch. There is a wide variance in weight between species, averaging between three and fourteen pounds, with a maximum weight of twenty pounds.

Preparation Suggestions: Rockfish is versatile and lends itself to several cooking methods: sautéing, frying, broiling, or grilling. We love rockfish in coconut milk or tomato-based stews like cioppino or in tacos with fresh cilantro and lime.

SHELLFISH

Alaska's variety of crab species can be easily boiled and enjoyed at a cookout or added to a variety of dishes from decadent breakfasts to special occasion dinners. Scallops, prized for their rich flavor and unique texture, are superb simply seared in butter or enjoyed over a salad.

DUNGENESS CRAB

Alaska is known for its large and flavorful Dungeness, prized for its sweet and tender, flaky white meat.

Season: Available frozen year-round

Harvest Method: Pot fishing

Size and Specs: Average weight is two to three pounds. Available whole or in leg clusters.

Preparation Suggestions: Store-bought crab comes precooked, so it is ready to eat. Just warm it by steaming in a large pot of boiling water or in the oven for 4 minutes to heat through. Dungeness is great dipped in butter or mixed into salads or pastas. We especially love making a morning omelet or eggs Benedict with Dungeness crab.

KING CRAB

This king of the sea has impressively meaty legs and a rich flavor that makes it a coveted delicacy among seafood lovers.

Season: Available frozen year-round

Harvest Method: Pot fishing

Size and Specs: Unmatched in size, quality, and appearance. Average weight is six to ten pounds. Available as individual legs and claws or leg clusters.

Preparation Suggestions: King crab comes precooked and extremely versatile for use in various recipes or enjoyment on its own. To warm, just it heat through for 4 minutes in a big pot of boiling water or in the oven. Enjoy with melted butter.

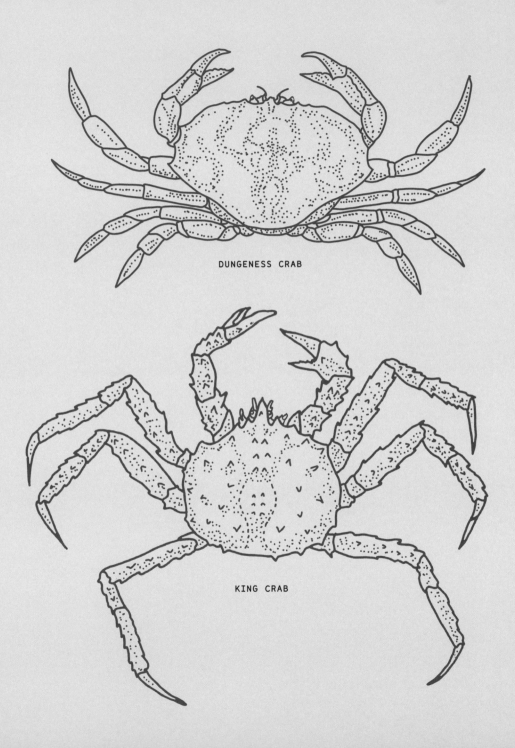

DUNGENESS CRAB

KING CRAB

SHELLFISH

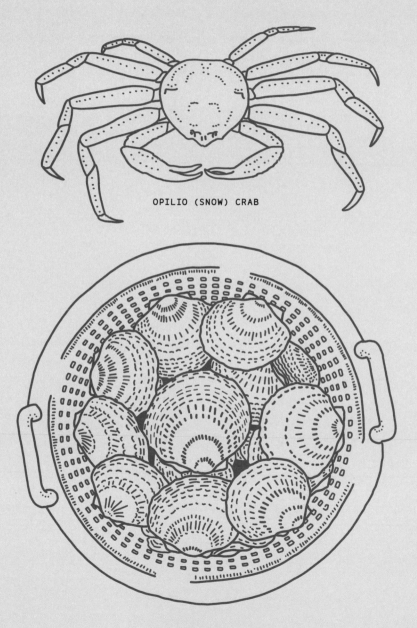

OPILIO (SNOW) CRAB

WEATHERVANE SCALLOPS

OPILIO CRAB

An elegant crab with a uniquely delicate and mild flavor, tender texture, and snow-white meat. Also called snow crab.

Season: Available frozen year-round

Harvest Method: Pot fishing

Size and Specs: Average weight is one to three pounds. Usually sold in leg clusters, but also available in cocktail claws, whole legs, or split legs.

Preparation Suggestions: Snow crab is sold precooked and ready to eat. To warm, heat it through for 4 minutes in a pot of boiling water or in the oven. Serve with melted butter as crab cakes, or fold the meat into an omelet.

WEATHERVANE SCALLOPS

Known for their mighty size and sweet, tender, buttery meat, weathervanes are the largest scallops in the world.

Season: Available frozen year-round

Harvest Method: Dredged by a carefully regulated fishery. Immediately hand-shucked and flash-frozen at sea for quality.

Size and Specs: Consistent in appearance, flavor, and texture, weathervanes are renowned for their large size, which is determined by the height of their shell (three to four inches at maturity).

Preparation Suggestions: Can be prepared in a variety of ways: grilled, sautéed, or pan-seared. Nothing is better than scallops seared in a hot pan with minced garlic, butter, and a sprinkle of sea salt and paired with a Caesar salad.

How to Fillet a Whole Fish

Buying and breaking down a whole fish may seem intimidating at first, but filleting is simple with the right approach, a sharp knife, and a little practice. Aside from being more economical and ensuring quality, buying a whole fish also gives you the bonus of cooking with all of its parts—from bones to skin—preventing waste and offering interesting new ingredients for you to cook with.

1 Under running water, rinse any excess slime from the fish's skin and lay it on its side on a large cutting board.

2 Using a sharp fillet knife, cut along the length of the fish's belly from anal fins to gills.

3 Make a crosswise cut just behind the gills from top to bottom, letting off before cutting through the backbone.

4 Cut the fillet free by running the knife along the fish's spine, from the gill end all the way to the tail, while holding on to the fish's head with your noncutting hand for leverage.

5 Once free, lay the fillet skin-side down and slip the knife under the rib bones that run along the belly (top) side. Gently cut the bones loose by following their angle.

6 If you want to remove the skin, make a crosswise nick near the tail, then run the knife between the meat and skin with a slight downward angle while holding on to the skin at the tail end with your non-cutting hand.

7 Run the back of the knife blade from gills to tail to reveal the pin bones. Pluck them out with pliers or tweezers.

8 Flip the fish over and repeat steps 3 through 7 to fillet the other half of the fish. Season, spice, and prepare for cooking.

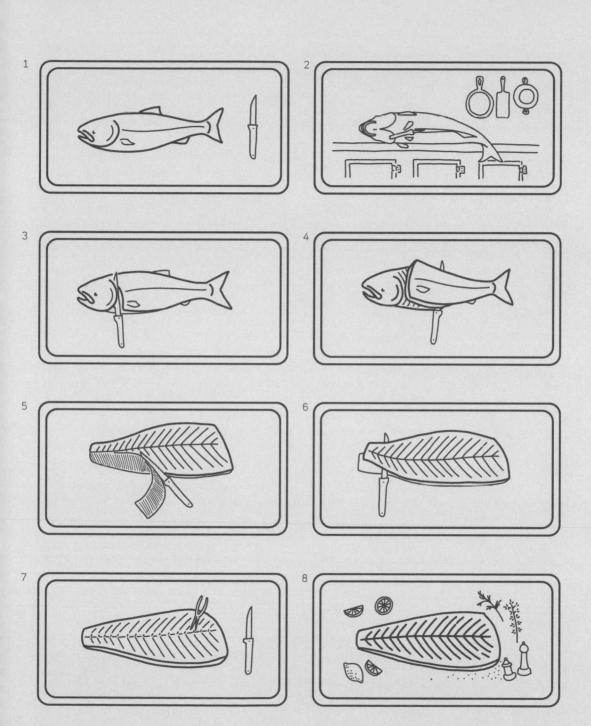

Wild Salmon Poke

When we're fishing we like to make giant bowls of poke with fresh sockeye to serve at back-deck dinner parties with friends on other boats. We remove the skin from the fillets, cut them into bite-size cubes, and freeze for twenty-four hours. Freezing is important to make the fish safe to eat raw; your home refrigerator's freezer will work great. When purchasing salmon, ensure that you are getting the best wild product by using your eyes and nose as a guide. Make sure that the fish looks firm and smells fresh (not "fishy").

MAKES 2 TO 4 SERVINGS

- 1 pound previously frozen wild sockeye salmon, skin and bones removed, cut into ½-inch cubes
- ¼ cup soy sauce
- 2 to 3 tablespoons freshly squeezed lime juice (from about 2 limes)
- 1 tablespoon toasted sesame oil
- 1 tablespoon rice vinegar
- 1 teaspoon sriracha or chili paste
- 3 tablespoons thinly sliced green onion
- 2 cloves garlic, minced
- 2 teaspoons toasted sesame seeds
- 2 teaspoons furikake seasoning (optional)
- 1 teaspoon finely grated fresh ginger
- 2 ripe avocados, sliced
- 2 (6-inch) Persian cucumbers, thinly sliced
- 4 cups steamed white or brown rice, for serving

Put the thawed cubed salmon in a medium bowl. In a small bowl, whisk together the soy sauce, lime juice, sesame oil, vinegar, sriracha, green onions, garlic, sesame seeds, furikake, and ginger until well combined. Pour the mixture over the salmon and fold it in gently to coat evenly.

Cover and chill the poke for at least 15 minutes. Serve with the avocado slices and cucumber over rice.

Sweet and Smoky Barbecued Salmon

Flavor your fish with a mouthwatering marinade before grilling it to perfection. The unmatched flavor of salmon fresh from the sea is enhanced by garlic, lemon, brown sugar, wood smoke, and sea salt. The fish can be grilled over coals on the beach or on a barbecue.

MAKES 6 TO 8 SERVINGS

- 1 cup soy sauce
- 1 cup packed dark brown sugar
- ¼ cup molasses
- ¼ cup vegetable oil
- Juice from 2 medium lemons (about 6 tablespoons)

- 8 cloves garlic
- 1 teaspoon flaky sea salt
- ½ teaspoon freshly ground black pepper
- 1 whole wild salmon, filleted with the skin on

Blend the soy sauce, sugar, molasses, oil, lemon juice, garlic, salt, and pepper in a blender until smooth. Pour the mixture over the salmon in a shallow glass dish or gallon ziplock bag. Marinate in the refrigerator for up to 8 hours.

When ready to cook, place the salmon fillets skin side down on a medium-high heat, well-greased grill. Cook for 10 minutes per inch of thickness, brushing with the marinade several times during grilling. Do not flip the fillets. Test doneness by flaking the fillets with a fork at their thickest part. Do not overcook.

Flavor Notes: We like to place a shallow flameproof pan of wood chips on the grill over the lowest flame setting to create a bit of a smoky outdoor campfire barbecue flavor. Alder is a common hardwood used for smoking salmon; it can be purchased in pellets, chopped chunks, or sawdust at most outdoor stores or online. We also like to soak cedar planks and grill the fish right on them for a similarly natural smokiness.

Smoked Salmon Frittata

with Goat Cheese, Cherry Tomatoes, and Chives

In our family's kitchen, salmon is eaten for breakfast, lunch, and dinner. This frittata is one of our favorite ways to start the day. Originating from Nina Burkholder's Grayback fish camp in Olga Bay, Alaska, this frittata makes for an easy lunch and even better leftovers. Look for hot-smoked salmon at your local fish counter or make your own. It is smoky, rich, and flaky, with enough moisture to pair with eggs. Serve slices of frittata over a handful of lightly dressed baby greens for a fresh morning meal.

MAKES 8 TO 10 SERVINGS

- 10 large eggs
- ¼ cup whole milk
- ¼ teaspoon kosher salt
- ¼ teaspoon freshly ground black pepper
- ½ pound hot-smoked wild salmon, broken into bite-size pieces

- 15 cherry tomatoes, halved
- 4 ounces fresh goat cheese, crumbled
- 1 bunch chives, chopped
- 1 tablespoon unsalted butter

Preheat the oven to 350 degrees F.

In a large bowl, whisk together the eggs, milk, salt, and pepper. Gently stir in the salmon, tomatoes, cheese, and chives.

Melt the butter in a large ovenproof frying pan over high heat. Pour the egg mixture into the pan and reduce the heat to medium. Cook for 1 minute, then transfer the pan to the oven and cook for 25 to 30 minutes, or until the center of the frittata is set and slightly puffed up. Let cool in the pan for 5 minutes before cutting into wedges for serving.

Smoked Salmon Spread

At lunchtime in grade school, it was always clear which kids came from fishing families. We all pulled sandwiches from our lunch boxes made from leftover salmon or halibut from the previous night's dinner, made into a quick spread (sometimes with onions or pickles or capers). This salmon spread is made with cream cheese, so it's a great complement to a toasted bagel, flatbread, or crackers. We usually use leftover, canned, or jarred smoked salmon for this recipe.

MAKES 2 TO 4 SERVINGS

- 1 (8-ounce) package cream cheese, softened
- 1 (6-ounce) can wild pink or sockeye salmon, drained, or 1 cup chopped smoked salmon
- 1 tablespoon minced red onion
- 1 clove garlic, minced
- 1 tablespoon freshly squeezed lemon juice
- Dash of cayenne
- Dash of freshly ground black pepper

Beat the cream cheese in a medium bowl with an electric mixer or by hand with a fork until smooth. Mix in the salmon, onion, garlic, lemon juice, cayenne, and black pepper. The spread can be stored in an airtight container in the refrigerator for up to 4 days.

Coconut Curry Fish Soup

This Thai-inspired coconut curry soup is comforting like a chowder but also light and alive with fresh lime juice, ginger, and cilantro. We love making it on the boat because the ingredients are simple and readily available, yet the flavor is fresh and tangy. Red curry paste (we used store-bought) brings the broth to life with its red chilies, coriander, lemongrass, garlic, and shallots. This soup is tasty made with salmon, halibut, rockfish, or shrimp—or throw in a combination! You can double the recipe for a big pot that will last you all week and add fresh garnishes to each bowl you enjoy. When we're fishing in Prince William Sound during the summer, we like to add fresh spot prawns that we caught and serve the soup over steaming white rice for an even heartier meal.

MAKES 6 TO 8 SERVINGS

- 2 tablespoons coconut oil
- ½ yellow onion, diced
- 3 to 4 cloves garlic, minced
- ½ cup red curry paste
- 1 tablespoon light brown sugar
- 2 (14-ounce) cans coconut milk
- 2½ cups fish, vegetable, or chicken stock
- ¼ cup freshly squeezed lime juice (from about 2 limes)
- ¼ cup finely chopped fresh ginger
- 2 tablespoons soy sauce
- 2 cups thinly sliced carrots
- 1½ cups chopped green beans
- 2 cups cubed wild skinless salmon, halibut, or rockfish, or whole shelled shrimp
- ½ cup fresh cilantro leaves, for garnish
- 2 limes, sliced, for garnish

Heat the oil in a large saucepan over medium-high heat. Add the onion and sauté until translucent. Add the garlic and sauté until lightly browned. Add the curry paste and cook for 1 minute, stirring constantly. Add the brown sugar and cook for 1 minute. Stir in the coconut milk, stock, lime juice, ginger, and soy sauce.

Reduce the heat to low, cover, and simmer for 30 minutes. Add the carrots and cook for 5 minutes. Add the green beans and cook for 5 more minutes, or until the vegetables are crisp-tender. Add the fish and cook for 2 minutes. Garnish the soup with cilantro and slices of lime.

Salmon and Avocado Eggs Benedict

Whip up this Benedict when you have some smoked salmon and ripe avocados. In Alaska, it is rare to find avocados that are the right kind of ripe—usually they are either rock hard or too soft because they have to travel so far to reach the state. So when fortune strikes and a friend from California visits, this is the right recipe to make for breakfast.

MAKES 2 SERVINGS

FOR THE HOLLANDAISE:
- ½ cup (1 stick) unsalted butter
- 2 large egg yolks
- 1 tablespoon freshly squeezed lemon juice
- 1 teaspoon Dijon mustard
- 1 teaspoon white wine vinegar
- Kosher salt and freshly ground black pepper

FOR THE EGGS:
- 1 teaspoon white wine vinegar
- 4 large whole eggs

FOR THE BENEDICT:
- 2 English muffins, sliced in half
- 1 ripe avocado, sliced
- 8 ounces smoked wild salmon lox, thinly sliced
- 1 tablespoon finely chopped fresh dill, for garnish

To make the hollandaise, melt the butter in a small pan over medium heat. Meanwhile, separate the egg yolks and place them in a heatproof bowl set over another small pan of simmering water. Gently whisk in the lemon juice and mustard. Very slowly whisk the melted butter into the egg mixture, stirring constantly until well combined. If needed, add a splash of water to loosen the sauce. Whisk in the vinegar and season the sauce with salt and pepper. Turn the heat off and keep warm over the pan of water, stirring occasionally, while you poach the eggs.

To poach the eggs, fill a small saucepan with 4 inches of water. Place over high heat until it reaches a light simmer and small bubbles begin to appear at the bottom of the pan. Stir in the vinegar. Swirl the simmering water with a slotted spoon to create a cyclone. Crack the eggs, one at a time, close to the swirling water and let them slip in gently. Cook the eggs for 4 minutes, or until the whites are cooked through but the yolks are still runny. Using a slotted spoon, carefully lift the poached eggs out of the saucepan and place them on a plate.

To make the Benedicts, toast the English muffins to a golden brown and place two halves on each plate. Top each half with a few slices of avocado, a thin layer of smoked salmon, a poached egg, a spoonful of hollandaise, and a pinch of dill. Repeat with the other muffins and serve immediately.

Salmon Gravlax
with Dijon-Dill Sauce

The village of False Pass near our homestead had only about fifty year-round inhabitants, a small store, one school, and a health clinic. Once or twice a year, a traveling doctor would visit the small communities on the Aleutian Islands. When we were young, the doctor's name was Pete—he heralded the news when our parents were pregnant with Emma, sold our dad his first fishing boat, and became a dear family friend. Eventually, his son worked on our boat, and his wife and daughter came to stay at Stonewall Place one summer. They introduced us to many Norwegian family recipes, including gravlax—raw salmon cured in salt, sugar, and dill. We make gravlax regularly while we're at sea, since fresh salmon are abundant and the hands-off preparation lends itself well to busy days on the back deck. It's wonderful served on cardamom bread, crackers, or a bagel with cream cheese, red onions, and capers.

MAKES 8 SERVINGS

FOR THE GRAVLAX:
- 3 tablespoons light brown sugar
- 1 tablespoon kosher salt
- 1 tablespoon freshly ground black pepper
- 2 skin-on wild salmon fillets
- Large bunch fresh dill

FOR THE SAUCE:
- ½ cup extra-virgin olive oil
- 2 tablespoons Dijon mustard
- 2 tablespoons minced fresh dill or 2 teaspoons dried
- 2 teaspoons granulated sugar

recipe continues

To make the gravlax, mix the brown sugar, salt, and pepper in a small bowl. Spread the rub on the flesh sides of the salmon fillets. (You can adjust the rub measurements as needed to generously cover the fillets.)

Place a generous amount of dill on the flesh of one fillet and set it in a 9-by-13-inch glass container. Lay the other fillet on top, flesh sides together. Place a small cutting board on the fillets, then weigh it down evenly with a couple of heavy cans, a large rock, or a brick. Tightly seal the container with a lid or plastic wrap and refrigerate for at least 24 hours. Pour off any liquids.

To make the sauce, stir together the olive oil and mustard, then add the dill and sugar. Mix until well blended.

To serve, scrape excess sugar from the salmon and slice it with an angled cut into very thin pieces. Top with the mustard sauce. Refrigerate any leftover sauce in a sealed container for up to one week.

Superfood Salmon Cakes

Our friend Jan has worked for many years as a commercial fisheries manager for the Alaska Department of Fish and Game, which is partly to say—she knows fish and she knows how to cook them. Jan's salmon cakes often fuel the women who play on her ice hockey team before tournaments and herself on long open-ocean swims, but yours might be the perfect protein-packed weeknight meal. These salmon cakes are our favorite way to give leftover salmon a second life, or to use the canned salmon in our pantry cupboards. Serve with the spicy dipping sauce for maximum enjoyment.

MAKES 4 TO 6 SERVINGS

- 1 tablespoon extra-virgin olive oil
- 1 medium yellow onion, diced
- 2 (15-ounce) cans wild pink or red salmon, or 4 cups cooked salmon, bones removed
- 1½ cups Italian bread crumbs, plus more for dredging
- ½ cup chopped fresh parsley
- 1 teaspoon kosher salt
- 1 teaspoon freshly ground black pepper

- 3 large eggs, beaten
- 1 tablespoon mayonnaise
- 1 tablespoon Dijon mustard
- 1 tablespoon Worcestershire sauce
- Vegetable oil, for frying

FOR THE DIPPING SAUCE:
- ½ cup mayonnaise
- 1 tablespoon Tiger Sauce or other favorite hot sauce

Heat the olive oil in a large frying pan over medium heat. Sauté the onion until translucent, then transfer to a small plate and set aside to cool. Wipe out the pan to reuse.

recipe continues

In a large bowl, mix together the salmon, bread crumbs, parsley, salt, pepper, and cooled onion. In a small bowl, whisk together the eggs, mayonnaise, mustard, and Worcestershire. Add the dressing to the salmon mixture. Form the mixture into ⅓-cup balls and then flatten into burger-shaped patties. Dredge in bread crumbs.

In the large frying pan, heat the vegetable oil. Carefully lower the salmon cakes into the hot oil, frying them until golden brown, about 3 minutes per side.

Meanwhile, make the spicy dipping sauce by mixing together the mayonnaise and Tiger Sauce in a small bowl. Serve with the salmon cakes.

Wild Superfood from the Sea

Here are some of the many reasons why eating wild Alaska seafood is so good for you.

Beautiful skin: Nutrients like vitamin B12, omega-3s, and vitamin A improve skin's elasticity and smoothness, and can help with dryness.

Sharp eyes: Omega-3s and vitamins A and D improve vision and prevent age-related macular degeneration.

Powerful brain: Vitamin B12 and high-quality protein protect brain cells and improve cognition and memory.

Strong bones: Vitamin E, omega-3s, and vitamin B12 keep bones strong by absorbing key nutrients to maintain density.

Healthy heart: Omega-3s reduce the chance of blood clots, heart attacks, and strokes.

Strong immune system: Vitamin E helps fight infection and boost immunity.

Good gut: Omega-3s reduce the effect of chronic digestive disorders.

Healthy joints: Omega-3s reduce the effects of rheumatoid arthritis.

Active bodies: Omega-3s and high-quality protein support athletic performance and recovery.

Healthy pregnancy: Omega-3s provide essential nutrients for mom and baby, and they advance fetal brain and eye development.

Smoked Salmon Sushi Hand Rolls

with Avocado and Cucumber

When we were three and four years old, we traveled with our parents and a group of Alaska fishermen to Japan. At that time, Japan was the biggest buyer of wild Alaska salmon, and fishermen like our parents wanted to learn more about the Japanese seafood industry, the companies buying our fish, and the people eating them. For several weeks we traveled to different cities, visiting local ports, fish markets, processing facilities, and sushi restaurants in each. Our parents were inspired by the food we ate in Japan—miso soup, sushi, sashimi, roe, and kelp became staples in our family's diet at Stonewall Place. These cone-shaped hand rolls are easy to assemble and fun to make with the whole family or guests. They can be packed with extra vegetables for added crunch.

MAKES 6 TO 8 SUSHI ROLLS

- 3 cups uncooked sushi rice
- 3¼ cups water
- Pinch of kosher salt
- 2 tablespoons seasoned rice vinegar
- 1 teaspoon toasted sesame seeds
- 8 ounces sliced shiitake mushrooms
- 1 tablespoon vegetable oil
- 1 teaspoon toasted sesame oil
- 1 teaspoon soy sauce, plus more for serving
- 1 red bell pepper, thinly sliced into 4-inch strips
- 1 cucumber, thinly sliced into 4-inch strips
- 2 ripe avocados, thinly sliced into 4-inch strips
- 1 pound wild smoked salmon, broken into chunks, or salmon lox, thinly sliced
- 1 (1-ounce) package nori sheets (about 10 sheets)
- Prepared wasabi or wasabi paste

Rinse the rice well until the water almost runs clear. Transfer to a medium pot with the water and salt. Bring to a boil, cover, and simmer over low heat for 20 minutes.

While the rice is still warm, transfer it to a large bowl and sprinkle with the vinegar. Using a wooden paddle or spatula, "slice" the rice to mix it up. Sprinkle with the sesame seeds and cover with plastic wrap or a damp kitchen towel. Let cool in the refrigerator.

In a medium frying pan over medium heat, sauté the mushrooms in the vegetable oil until tender, about 5 minutes. Add the sesame oil and cook for 2 more minutes. Season with the soy sauce, then transfer to a small serving bowl.

Place the bell pepper, cucumber, and avocado into individual bowls. Place the salmon on a small plate.

Cut the nori sheets in half to make two rectangles from each sheet.

Once all ingredients are ready and immediately before serving, assemble the hand rolls. On a flat surface, place a nori sheet horizontally in front of you, rough side up. Spread sushi rice (either using wet fingers or the back of a spoon) on the left half of the sheet, leaving a ½-inch border; there should be 2 to 3 inches without rice on the right half. Align the vegetable strips on top of the rice diagonally, with the ends pointing toward the upper left corner of the sheet. Top the line of veggies with the salmon and mushrooms.

To fold the roll, start with the left bottom corner of nori, folding it up over the ingredients, and then wrap the right side over and around it to form a cone about the size of a sugar cone. Seal with a dab of water on the nori seam. Serve immediately with soy sauce and wasabi.

The Stonewall Smokehouse

A summertime portrait of our mother: Fleece jacket (sewn on her serger) under orange rain bibs over brown Xtratuf boots, all covered in fish scales. Pushing the wind-teased wisps of her blond hair back with the inside of her forearm, bare hands covered in brown sugar, salt, and salmon blood. A white-handled fillet knife gripped in one hand, the tail of a sockeye in the other, cutting long strips from a fillet at her fish-cleaning table. If there is something our mom loves most about living in Alaska, smoking salmon might be it.

Traditionally in the Aleutians, salmon is smoked in fillets left on the tail and hung over poles or beams in a smokehouse, but our mom loved smoking king salmon, and their thick fillets and high oil content make it difficult to dry out. She began smoking fish using her own technique: cutting the fillets into half-inch-wide strips, tying them together with string, and hanging them to dry as individual pieces. This method meant that she could utilize the whole fish without waste and ended up with a product caramelized in rich salmon oil, salt, and sugar and dried by the perfect combination of wind and smoke.

Before starting on a batch of smoked salmon, we ventured out in the skiff to collect driftwood on neighboring shores to use for the smokehouse fire. Mom walked the beach with a pocketknife, gouging the bark of logs to see if they had the spongy texture of cottonwood, her favorite flavor of smoke that had floated in from hundreds of miles away. If they were right, we rolled the logs down the beach and lifted them into the skiff to take home, where we would chainsaw them into smaller pieces and stack them on the wood pile in preparation for the barrel stove.

The next step was to clean the salmon she caught in her beach setnet, cutting away the rib bones and stripping the salmon into long, thin pieces while holding their tails. The strips were

soaked in a sea-salt-and-brown-sugar brine in plastic totes amid
the beach grass. After brining, we carried the salmon strips down
the beach to the smokehouse. We used the top of our cedar hot tub
as a tying station-securing two equal-sized strips of salmon
together with a bit of string and hanging them over long poles
resting on five-gallon buckets. This process took a full day, with
a few breaks for an orange from the root cellar, a cup of tea up
at the house, or a chocolate bar. But someone always had to stand
guard in case a hungry raven, fox, or bear wandered down the beach
and found our hard work.

      Fishermen and villagers who tasted our mom's smoked salmon
loved it and traded her wild birds, game, shellfish, or sometimes
a good book or the latest newspaper flown in from Anchorage for a
bag full of the strips. The village had its own barter system that
helped the region's bounty make it into each family's home. Mom
also gave her smoked salmon to friends in the village who didn't
have their own smokehouses, so they could enjoy the flavors of
salt, sea, and smoke too.

Stonewall Cold-Smoked Salmon Strips

This recipe requires a smokehouse, whole fresh salmon, cottonwood, and a stretch of dry breezy weather, so it may not be accessible to everyone using this cookbook; however, it feels too important to leave out. Read on to understand the process of smoking salmon the way our family always has—in our mom's voice.

- Fresh whole wild salmon
- Kosher salt (we use Morton Coarse Kosher Salt)
- Dark brown sugar
- Twine
- Clean newspaper or cardboard

- Smokehouse
- Very sharp fillet knife
- Cottonwood
- A stretch of dry breezy weather

Clean the salmon. While filleting it, keep each side attached to the tail. If using kings or large chums, thin the fillets to about 1 inch thick. Reserve the trimmed flesh for canning or freezing. Hold on to the tail and cut the fillets lengthwise into ½-inch strips. The strips can be thinner but not thicker, or they will not cure and dry out properly. Cut the strips from the tail (which can be discarded, composted, or used for stock).

In a large clean plastic tote or bucket, make a salt brine with a ratio of 1 cup of salt for every gallon of water. Place the salmon strips into the salt brine for 12 minutes, stirring the strips every 4 minutes to ensure even brining. The strips will firm up. Remove them from the brine but do not rinse. Place the strips in a slotted basket to drain for 10 minutes.

Put the strips in a clean container and add brown sugar—I use about 3 cups sugar per 2½ gallons salmon strips. Using clean hands, spread the sugar onto the strips. The sugar will dissolve and create a sticky glaze.

Cut twine into 1-foot lengths. Tie a salmon strip on to each end by securing the twine about 2 inches from the end of each strip. Tie it tight enough so the twine is slightly biting into the salmon flesh, but beware that if you tie the string too tight (to the skin), the salmon will end up on the ground in a day or so.

Place the newspaper or cardboard on the smokehouse floor; should any strips fall, they will stay clean and can be rehung. Hang the strips in the smokehouse or another fly-free space so there is air circulation for the flesh on the strips to dry to the touch. If the weather is windy and sunny, this can happen in the smokehouse with the side vents open. You can also do this in a garage with fans.

recipe continues

Air-dry the strips until pellicle, a tacky outer layer, forms, then transfer the strips to the smoker. Space the strips over the racks strung across the eves and separate them by a couple of inches to ensure proper air and smoke circulation.

To smoke the salmon, cut cottonwood to the length of the stove and keep a pile of wood close by. The point of cold-smoking is to cure and add smoky flavor to the fish, not to cook it. I fill a couple of five-gallon buckets with water and soak pieces of cottonwood until I need it for smoking.

You must use cold smoke and fire to successfully smoke salmon this way. If your fire is too hot, the fish will cook and all your hard work will be found on the smokehouse floor. I get a small dry fire going with the smokehouse sides open, make sure there are good coals, add three to four pieces of wet cottonwood, and then close up the smoker and let it do its magic. I keep the fire gently stoked throughout the day, checking that there's always gentle smoke coming off it.

During the first few days of smoking, work through the salmon strips every day. Separate those that may be sticking together, or move them around in the smoker so they get equal amounts of smoke exposure. The length of the smoking process depends on the weather, salmon species, and strip thickness. It may take from one to two weeks for a batch to be ready.

When the salmon is no longer raw in the middle and the strips are stiff, remove the strips from the racks and cut off the twine. The tied ends make great snacks or dog treats. Cut the strips into desired lengths and store in vacuum-packed bags in the freezer. If vacuum-packed, the smoked salmon will last for up to a year in the freezer.

Jarred Smoked Salmon Strips

After smoking for three days and nights, salmon strips are perfect for jarring. Jarring smoked salmon is great way to keep it over the winter rather than freezing, and gives it a unique flavor and texture that's perfect for salmon dip, frittatas, or salmon cakes. Set aside a full afternoon to jar your smoked salmon, which will leave you with beautiful capsules of summer abundance. You will need a large pressure cooker and pint-size wide-mouth glass jars with lids. This recipe comes from Glady Evanoff's fish camp on Lake Clark. You can find additional canning resources online through Alaska Sea Grant (AlaskaSeaGrant.org).

- Salmon strips smoked for 3 days and nights (see page 74)
- Wide-mouth pint canning jars
- Extra-virgin olive oil
- Dark brown sugar

Cut the salmon strips into pieces that stand comfortably inside the pint jars, being sure to leave at least 1 inch of headroom. Pack the jars with strips and add about 1 tablespoon brown sugar and 2 tablespoons oil into each. Wipe the jar necks clean and secure with the lids.

Place the jars in a pressure cooker and process according to manufacturer's instructions for 100 minutes at 10 pounds of pressure.

Check the lids for a proper seal and tighten the bands as needed. Label the jars and store in a cool, dry pantry for up to 12 months.

Pickled Salmon

This traditional recipe is made with hearty chunks of salmon and succulent onion slices, similar to the pickled herring that is common to Scandinavian coastal cuisine. Pickling is one popular way people preserve salmon in western Alaska. In False Pass, villagers salted silver salmon they harvested in the fall to trade the cannery store for credit to buy groceries over the winter. Jars of pickled fish were also made from the salted fish and traded for smoked fish, a halibut fillet, or a piece of caribou meat. Enjoy pickled salmon on sesame crackers or straight from the jar.

1 QUART-SIZED JAR OF PICKLED SALMON

- Pickling salt
- 2 pounds boneless, skinless wild salmon fillets
- Apple cider vinegar or white vinegar
- Sugar
- Pickling spice
- 2 white onions, thinly sliced
- 1 quart-size glass canning jar

Sprinkle a thin layer of salt in a deep, clean bucket or large baking pan, then arrange a single layer of salmon fillets on top. Pour more salt over the fish to cover, then another layer of fillets, and so on, alternating fish and salt, making sure that all fish is well covered in salt. The salt will help cure the fish and draw out moisture. Cover and refrigerate for 24 hours.

To make the pickling liquid, combine 2 parts vinegar to 1 part sugar and 1 tablespoon pickling spice in a saucepan over low heat. Simmer for 5 minutes, stirring occasionally. Refrigerate the liquid until cool.

After 24 hours, remove the fillets from the salt and rinse under cold running water. Discard the salt. Return the salmon to the rinsed container, add enough water (tap water is fine) to cover the fish, and refrigerate overnight.

After 8 to 10 hours, remove the fillets from the water and pat dry. Cut into bite-size chunks (about 1-inch cubes).

In a quart-size glass jar (or other nonmetallic container), add the onion pieces and salmon chunks in alternating 2-inch layers, then pour some pickling liquid over the top. Layer more onions and salmon, pouring liquid over them, until all are used up or the jar is full (with 1-inch headspace). Be sure there is sufficient pickling liquid in the jar to cover all layers.

Seal and refrigerate for a minimum of 72 hours for proper pickling, but you can marinate longer for more intense flavor. Label the jar and store in the refrigerator for up to 1 month.

Fishing Knots

A skilled fisherman knows knots that help make work easier on the water. These knots are used to tie a boat to the dock, lash a buoy to the boat's rail, fasten lines together, or lift something heavy from the dock. They come in handy every day and can be learned with a little practice.

SQUARE KNOT

A simple way to connect two lines or to join the ends of a single line to bind around an object. The knot is formed by tying a right-handed overhand knot and then a left-handed overhand knot, or vice versa (as the saying goes: "right over left, left over right, makes a knot both tidy and tight").

CLOVE HITCH

Handy for temporary fastening, such as tying up to a piling or lashing buoys to a rail. For stronger hold or longer periods of time, add half hitches after tying the clove hitch.

BOWLINE

The most-used knot by fishermen. An essential multipurpose knot that can be tied quickly and easily. Used to tie two lines together, and a good way to make a fixed loop that can be used for hitching, fastening, mooring, or lifting. Easy to untie after it has been tightened or strained by a heavy load.

BOWLINE ON A BIGHT

A knot that makes a pair of secure fixed-size loops in the middle of a rope that do not slip; easy to untie after it has been tightened or strained by a heavy load.

FIGURE EIGHT

Traditionally a climbing knot. This stopper knot forms a strong, secure, nonslip loop at the end of a rope that is easy to visually inspect. It's also known as a Flemish Bend.

SHEET BEND

Effective for joining lines of different weight or construction, and quick and easy to tie and untie. This knot easily works loose when not under load. For extra security, add another turn in the smaller end, making a double sheet bend. Commonly used by longliners.

CARRICK BEND

Used for joining two lines, this knot is appropriate for heavy rope or cable that is too large or stiff to form into other knots like crab line. Its beautiful, symmetrical, interwoven shape also lends itself well to decorative purposes. Commonly used by pot fishermen.

CLEATING HITCH

Used to tie a boat up to the dock or to another boat by attaching a line between fixed cleats on the boat's rail. The cleating hitch is tied by wrapping the line around the base of the cleat in a figure-eight shape, then forming one or more half hitches around the cleat's horns to secure it.

MONKEY FIST

Named after its resemblance to a small bunched fist or paw. It is tied at the end of a rope to serve as a weight, making it easier to throw. It is also used as an ornamental knot.

Crispy Beer-Battered Halibut

Our dad's favorite way to eat fish—fried! There's something about the oily crunch of this beer-battered halibut when it's cooked to a perfect golden brown and dipped into a favorite sauce that is hard to beat. This recipe is simple, fun to cook with friends, and can be made with any firm fish. We cook halibut, cod, rockfish, and salmon this way. Pair it with Crunchy Green Cabbage Salad (page 143).

MAKES 2 GENEROUS SERVINGS

- Vegetable or peanut oil, for frying
- 2 cups all-purpose flour, plus more for dredging
- 1 teaspoon kosher salt
- 1 large egg, beaten
- 18 ounces beer, preferably amber
- 1 cup panko bread crumbs
- 1 pound firm fish, skin removed, cut into 2-by-3-inch pieces
- 1/2 cup homemade aioli or tartar sauce, for serving

In a deep pot, heat 1 inch of oil to 375 degrees F.

Meanwhile, in a shallow bowl, mix together the flour, salt, egg, and beer until it's the consistency of runny pancake batter.

Arrange a shallow plate of flour for dredging, the beer batter, and a shallow plate of panko in a line on a work surface.

Dip each piece of fish in flour, batter, then panko and transfer to a clean plate. Deep-fry the fish, a few pieces at a time, in the hot oil until golden brown, 2 to 3 minutes. Do not overcrowd the pan, or the fish will not crisp properly.

Carefully remove each piece of fish from the oil with a slotted spoon or tongs and let rest on clean newspaper or paper towels to drain. Once all the fish is cooked, serve with your sauce of choice.

Halibut Ceviche

This ceviche recipe was passed down to his sons by Kevin Bell, an Alaskan captain who sailed on the Alaska Maritime National Wildlife Refuge's research vessel, the M/V *Tiglax*, to the westernmost reaches of the Aleutian Islands. He passed his love for the sea on to his sons, one who works on Alaska's ferries and one who captains a fishing boat. Cured in lime juice with a kick of jalapeño and fresh cilantro, this ceviche will feed a happy crowd. Shrimp can be substituted if preferred.

MAKES 4 TO 6 SERVINGS

- 3 pounds halibut, skin removed, cut into ½-inch cubes
- Juice from 6 limes (about ¾ cup)
- 8 medium carrots, finely chopped
- 2 medium green bell peppers, finely chopped
- 2 medium tomatoes, finely chopped
- 1 red onion, finely chopped
- 2 jalapeños, minced
- 1 (6-ounce) can black olives, finely chopped
- 1 cup virgin olive oil
- 1 cup dry white wine
- 1 bunch fresh cilantro, minced
- 1 tablespoon minced fresh oregano
- 1 tablespoon minced fresh parsley
- Kosher salt
- Ground white pepper

Place the halibut cubes in a large shallow dish, and pour lime juice over the top. Let sit for 15 minutes.

In a large bowl, combine the carrots, bell peppers, tomatoes, onion, jalapeños, and black olives and toss to combine. Drain the lime juice from the halibut and transfer it to the bowl. Stir gently until the ingredients are mixed. Carefully fold in the oil, wine, cilantro, oregano, and parsley. Season to taste with salt and pepper. Serve with tortilla chips and slices of fresh avocado.

Sautéed Halibut
with Lemon-Pesto Butter

We used to spend the afternoons jigging for halibut from our mom's skiff in Ikatan Bay, sometimes bringing home a forty- to hundred-pound fish that would feed our family for many meals. One reason we love halibut so much is that it's incredibly versatile but also easy to cook. This recipe is a good example of how tasty it can be with a simple preparation—all you really need is halibut, butter, herbs, and a good pan. Paired with lemon or pesto pasta, this is one of our family's favorite weekday dinners.

MAKES 4 TO 6 SERVINGS

- 3 tablespoons unsalted butter, softened, plus 1 tablespoon for coating the pan
- 1 tablespoon homemade or store-bought pesto
- 1½ teaspoons finely chopped fresh basil
- 1 teaspoon finely chopped shallots
- ½ teaspoon grated lemon zest
- 6 (4-ounce) skinless halibut portions
- 2 teaspoons flaky sea salt
- 1 teaspoon freshly ground black pepper

Combine the butter, pesto, basil, shallots, and lemon zest in a small saucepan over low heat, stirring until the butter is melted and all is well blended.

Heat a large cast-iron pan over medium-high heat. Sprinkle the halibut evenly on both sides with the salt and pepper. Coat the pan with butter. Once melted, add the halibut and cook for 5 minutes on each side. Test doneness by cutting into the center of a fillet with a knife. The fish should flake apart and appear opaque white, not translucent. Pour the lemon-pesto butter over the fish before serving.

Halibut Chowder

This classic creamy chowder is one of our favorite recipes to make on the boat because we always have canned corn, onions, and potatoes, and we can throw in our freshest fish to make a great pot of hot stew to warm the crew. We love halibut because of its extra-firm texture, but cod, rockfish, or salmon are delicious too.

MAKES 8 TO 10 SERVINGS

- ½ pound bacon, diced
- 2 cups diced celery
- 1 cup chopped yellow onion
- 4 cups cubed Yukon gold potatoes
- 1 teaspoon kosher salt
- 1 teaspoon freshly ground black pepper
- 8 cups water

- 2 cups chicken stock
- 1 (15-ounce) can creamed corn
- 1 tablespoon dried thyme
- 2 cups heavy whipping cream
- 1⅓ pounds halibut, cod, rockfish, or wild salmon, skin removed, cut into 1-inch cubes (about 4 cups)

In a Dutch oven over medium heat, fry the bacon until crispy. Transfer to a plate and set aside.

Sauté the celery and onions in the same pot over medium heat. Add the potatoes, salt, and pepper; cover with the water and cook until the potatoes are tender, about 15 minutes. Add the stock, creamed corn, and thyme, and bring to a simmer. Stir in the cream and heat through. Do not boil or the stew will curdle.

Add the cubed fish and simmer for 2 minutes, then turn off the burner and let sit for 5 minutes. Ladle into bowls and garnish with the bacon.

Creamy Parmesan-Baked Halibut

with Spinach

Alaska comfort food—the world's premium whitefish baked with creamy spinach, Parmesan, lemon, and a little fresh parsley and white pepper. We make this dish to warm the crew up on chilly days at sea. It's an easy-to-cook, easy-to-eat crowd-pleaser—kids love it too!

MAKES 4 TO 6 SERVINGS

- 3 pounds halibut, cut into 6 equal portions
- 4 cups dry white wine (or enough to cover)
- 5 cups packed fresh spinach
- 1¼ cups grated Parmesan cheese, divided
- ½ to ¾ cup sour cream
- 2 teaspoons ground white pepper
- 1 large lemon, sliced
- ½ cup fresh parsley leaves, for garnish

In a large shallow dish or ziplock bag, soak the halibut in the wine for 1 hour. Remove and pat dry with paper towels.

Preheat the oven to 375 degrees F. Grease a 9-by-13-inch baking dish and set aside.

Bring a large pot of water to a steady boil. Submerge the spinach in the water and blanch until the stems are no longer rigid, about 40 seconds, Drain and transfer the spinach to a bowl of ice water to stop cooking. Drain.

Stir 1 cup of the Parmesan, the sour cream, and the white pepper into the spinach. Spread in the bottom the baking dish. Arrange the halibut on top of the spinach mixture. Place a lemon slice on top of each piece of fish, then sprinkle evenly with the remaining ¼ cup of Parmesan.

Bake for 10 to 15 minutes depending on thickness. Sprinkle with the parsley leaves just before serving.

Cucumber-Dill Sauce for Fish

Usually we cook fish with just a little butter, sea salt, and lemon squeezed on top because this simple combination of ingredients brings out a fish's true flavors. But sometimes the right sauce can offer an entirely new dimension to your meal, and this is one we make in the late summertime when the cucumbers ripen in our garden. We love the sauce on salmon, halibut, and Pacific cod, but it is also tasty on rice-and-bean bowls, fish or chicken tacos, and fresh poke.

MAKES ABOUT 2 CUPS

- ¼ cup (½ stick) unsalted butter
- 1 medium English cucumber, peeled, seeded, and chopped into ¼-inch pieces
- ¼ cup chopped white onion
- 2 tablespoons chicken broth
- 1 cup sour cream
- 1 tablespoon fresh dill, or 1 teaspoon dried
- 1 teaspoon Kosher salt
- ½ teaspoon freshly ground black pepper

Melt the butter in a medium saucepan over low heat. Add the cucumber, onion, and chicken broth. Cover and cook for about 10 minutes, stirring occasionally, until the cucumber is tender—do not overcook or the green color will be lost.

Transfer the mixture to a blender and puree until smooth. Add the sour cream, dill, and salt and pepper to taste. Pour the sauce back into the pan and keep warm until ready to serve over your fish of choice. Leftover sauce can be covered, stored in the refrigerator, and reheated as desired for up to 2 days.

Beurre Blanc for Fish

This sauce made from wine, butter, and garlic will complement your favorite fish—whether grilled, broiled, or pan-fried. We love drizzling it over grilled or broiled salmon, with a side of smashed garlic potatoes and fresh greens.

MAKES 2 GENEROUS SERVINGS

- ½ cup dry white wine
- 3 tablespoons finely chopped shallots or chives
- 1 clove garlic, minced
- Dash of ground white pepper
- ½ cup (1 stick) unsalted butter

In a small saucepan, combine the wine, shallots, garlic, and white pepper. Very carefully reduce the liquid over medium heat until almost dry, but without scorching the pan.

Add the butter and increase the heat to high. Using a whisk or fork, quickly stir in a circular motion. When the butter is half melted, remove the pan from the heat and continue stirring until the steam stops and the sauce thickens. Pour over your fish of choice. Leftovers can be stored in an airtight container and refrigerated for up to one week.

Furikake Seaweed Seasoning

Wade, who worked as a crewman on our boat for most of our child-hood, brought furikake from his home in Hawaii to the boat each sum-mer to shake over the fish we ate at sea. Fish and rice with a green salad from the garden has always been our family's go-to meal, especially in the summertime, when the salmon are running and the garden grows wild under long days of sunlight. White or brown rice completes the meal with soy or teriyaki sauce. The seasoning we shake on top is a dried seaweed and sesame seed blend that you can find in most grocery stores or Asian food markets, but it can also be easily made at home. All you need is a mortar and pestle or coffee grinder, a few sheets of nori seaweed, sesame seeds, salt, and sugar. It's nice on rice, noodles, vegetables, eggs, buttered popcorn, and poke.

MAKES ABOUT 1 CUP

- 4 sheets nori seaweed
- ½ cup toasted white and/or black sesame seeds, divided
- 1 teaspoon sugar
- 1 teaspoon coarse flaky sea salt

Slowly wave each sheet of nori over a low flame or stovetop burner until toasted and crisp. Cut the toasted sheets into small shreds with scissors.

Using a mortar and pestle, grind together ¼ cup of the sesame seeds, the sugar, and the salt. Stir in the nori and the remaining ¼ cup of ses-ame seeds (do not grind). Sprinkle over your fish of choice. Store in an airtight glass spice jar or container for up to 6 months.

King Crab Bisque

This is a rich and seriously creamy bisque thick with Alaska's finest crabmeat. We often traded crab fishermen passing by our homestead a homemade pie for a few legs of fresh king crab. This recipe is our favorite way to enjoy this bounty from the Bering Sea, but any other crab can be substituted with similar results. Serve it with fresh sourdough bread and butter.

MAKES 8 SERVINGS

- ½ cup (1 stick) unsalted butter
- 2 cups diced celery
- 1 cup diced yellow onion
- 4 cups whole milk
- 3 cups chicken stock
- 2 cups heavy cream
- 1 teaspoon ground white pepper
- ½ teaspoon kosher salt
- 3 tablespoons cornstarch
- 3 tablespoons water
- 1½ pounds crabmeat, removed from shells
- Fresh chives, chopped
- Pinch of paprika

Heat the butter in a large saucepan over medium heat. Add the celery and onion and sauté until tender. Stir in the milk, chicken stock, cream, white pepper, and salt. Bring to boil, then reduce the heat to a simmer.

Create a slurry by whisking together the cornstarch in the water until dissolved. Stir it into the soup and simmer for another 2 minutes, until thickened. Add the crabmeat and then turn off heat—the heat of the broth will warm it through. Garnish with the chives and paprika.

Creamy Crab and Artichoke Dip

Bring this hot crab dip to your next potluck or dinner party and prepare to be remembered forever. It's rich and creamy with a hint of spice and a lot of love. We make it for holidays and other special occasions because it feels celebratory with its crabby, cheesy decadence. Break out a warm baguette and spread this on top.

MAKES 8 SERVINGS

- 1 cup sour cream
- ½ cup mayonnaise
- 4 ounces cream cheese, softened
- 1½ pounds crabmeat
- 2 (10-ounce) jars oil-packed artichokes, drained and finely chopped
- 1 yellow onion, minced
- ½ cup grated Parmesan cheese, divided

- 2 tablespoons chopped fresh parsley
- 1 tablespoon hot sauce, such as Tabasco
- ½ teaspoon kosher salt
- 1 teaspoon freshly ground black pepper
- 2 tablespoons chopped green chilies (optional)
- Bread crumbs, for topping

Preheat the oven to 350 degrees F. Butter a 9-by-9-inch casserole dish and set aside.

In a medium mixing bowl, whip the sour cream, mayonnaise, and cream cheese together. Add the crabmeat, artichokes, onion, Parmesan (minus 3 tablespoons), parsley, hot sauce, salt, pepper, and green chilies, if you like extra spice! Mix well.

Spoon the mixture into the casserole dish and top with the bread crumbs and reserved 3 tablespoons Parmesan. Bake for 15 to 20 minutes, or until golden brown.

King Crab Cakes

When we have king crab in our kitchen, it's rare that we don't eat all the legs with melted butter in one sitting. However, if we are lucky enough to have leftovers, we make crab omelets for breakfast and crab cakes for lunch. These tender, savory, crispy cakes taste great dipped in garlic aioli or sriracha mayo. Though we love to use king crab here, the cakes can be made with whatever crabmeat you fancy. Pair them with the Kale Caesar Salad with Avocado Dressing (page 148) or your favorite fresh greens.

MAKES 4 TO 6 SERVINGS

- ¼ cup (½ stick) unsalted butter
- 1 medium yellow onion, chopped
- ½ cup bread crumbs
- 1 pound crabmeat
- 3 large eggs, beaten
- 2 tablespoons chopped fresh parsley
- 2 tablespoons chopped green onion
- 1 teaspoon kosher salt
- 1 teaspoon dry mustard powder
- 2 to 4 tablespoons heavy cream, for binding
- All-purpose flour, for dredging
- Butter or vegetable oil, for frying

Melt the butter in a large cast-iron frying pan over medium heat and cook the onion until just transparent. Transfer the onion to a mixing bowl and add the bread crumbs, blending well. Mix in the crabmeat, eggs, parsley, green onions, salt, and mustard powder. Add just enough cream to bind everything together.

Shape the mixture into flat cakes 3 to 4 inches wide. Fill a shallow dish with flour and roll each cake in it before frying. Fry the cakes in butter or oil in the same pan used to cook the onions (wiped clean) over medium-high heat until nicely browned on both sides and cooked through, about 3 minutes each side.

Boat Letters

Because Alaska is big, the water is wide, and modern modes of communication are challenging while at sea, always bring some envelopes, stamps, and writing paper on board. Find a bucket to sit on outside in a patch of sun and out of the wind, in the boat's wheelhouse, or somewhere where you can look out to the horizon and think and write without interruption. If the forecast is gray, you can always don rain gear and pull out a Rite in the Rain notebook—wet weather doesn't need to stop you.

Life at sea can be physically and mentally trying; it can also be inspiring, defining, and at times indescribable to those who haven't experienced the beautiful wilds of Alaska's oceans themselves. To us, writing sometimes feels like the best way to tell these stories because we allow ourselves the time to sit down and reflect on our day-to-day experiences. It helps us make sense of the best moments and the worst, the soreness in our bodies, the thoughts and dreams that occupy our minds day in and day out, the plans we have stowed away for our next visit to land, and the people we love and miss.

Writing and receiving boat letters has always been a special exchange between our fishing friends. Without telephones or internet, hundreds of miles apart, living and working with our families, we have stayed connected through boat letters. It took weeks for a letter to travel from our homestead on the Alaska Peninsula to our friend's fish camp in Bristol Bay or our pen pals in southeast Alaska, passing from the hands of the post office clerk to the bush plane pilot, to the cannery office and tender and fishing boat. Reading news from a faraway friend and seeing familiar handwriting on a well-traveled envelope brings great comfort, knowing someone is thinking about you from across the sea.

Spicy Seafood Cioppino

Experience the ocean's freshest delicacies with our mom's favorite fish stew. Originating in San Francisco, this Italian American dish was traditionally made from the cold and salty Pacific Ocean's catch of the day stewed with juicy fresh tomatoes in a wine sauce. Our mom's recipe pulls in Alaska's seasonal shellfish, halibut, crab, and shrimp. The beautiful thing about it is seafood can be substituted according to seasonal availability. This dish calls for store-bought arrabbiata pasta sauce as the base, which is typically made with tomatoes, garlic, and spicy red peppers cooked in olive oil. Serve the stew with crusty, buttery, toasted sourdough bread for dipping and prolonging the rich flavors of the sea.

MAKES 6 TO 8 SERVINGS

- 3 tablespoons extra-virgin olive oil
- 1 large yellow onion (or 3 shallots), diced
- 1 medium fennel bulb, thinly sliced
- 2 stalks celery, chopped
- 2 large carrots, diced
- 4 cloves garlic, roughly chopped
- 2 teaspoons kosher salt
- ½ teaspoon freshly ground black pepper
- 1 (24-ounce) jar arrabbiata sauce
- 1½ cups dry white wine
- 6 cups fish or chicken stock
- 1 bay leaf

- Fish sauce, clam juice, or anchovy paste, for seasoning (optional)
- 1 pound manila clams, scrubbed
- 1 pound mussels, scrubbed and debearded
- 1 pound firm fish, such as halibut or salmon, skin removed, cut into bite-size pieces
- ½ pound scallops or large shrimp, peeled and deveined
- ½ pound crab legs or prawns (optional)
- ¼ to ½ cup chopped fresh parsley

recipe continues

Heat the oil in a large, heavy-bottomed pot or Dutch oven over medium heat. Add onion and fennel and sauté for 5 minutes, stirring occasionally. Add the celery, carrots, and garlic and continue sautéing for 5 more minutes. Season with the salt and pepper. Add the arrabbiata and wine. Bring the liquid to a simmer and allow it to reduce by half before adding the stock and bay leaf. Taste and adjust the seasoning. If you would like to create more depth in the broth (especially if using chicken stock), add a splash of fish sauce, a small bottle of clam juice, or even a few teaspoons of anchovy paste.

Once the carrots are tender, the broth is ready. It will take about 10 minutes to cook the seafood, so the broth can rest on the stovetop until just before serving. You could also make it ahead of time, refrigerate it, and reheat at mealtime.

Add the clams, mussels, fish, scallops, and any other seafood to the pot. Cook for 10 minutes, or until the clams and mussels have opened and the fish is cooked through. Ladle the stew into bowls, garnish with the parsley, and serve with crusty buttered bread.

Paella

with Chicken, Shrimp, and Mussels

Our mom taught herself how to make paella after bringing home a giant paella pan from a trip to Europe. She brings it out when friends fill her kitchen, to delight them with this spectacular seafood and rice dish. Friends and family give her saffron for her birthdays in hopes that this gesture will keep the paella cooking. Paella is a dish that shows off its ingredients against a bed of vibrant yellow saffron rice—whether it's shrimp, chicken, scallops, mussels, clams, or sausage. It's a complete meal in a pan and delightful to watch simmer on the stovetop while sharing a bottle of white wine in the kitchen.

MAKES 6 TO 8 SERVINGS

- ¼ cup water
- ½ teaspoon saffron threads
- 1¾ cups arborio rice
- 16 debearded mussels or steamer clams, scrubbed
- 6 tablespoons extra-virgin olive oil, divided
- 6 to 8 bone-in, skin-on chicken thighs, excess fat trimmed
- 5 ounces chorizo sausage, casings removed, cut into ¼-inch slices
- 2 large yellow onions, chopped

- 4 large cloves garlic, crushed
- 1 teaspoon paprika
- 3½ ounces chopped green beans or ¾ cup frozen peas
- 5 cups fish, chicken, or vegetable stock
- 1 teaspoon kosher salt
- Freshly ground black pepper
- 16 raw shrimp, peeled but tails left on
- 1 red bell pepper, chopped
- Chopped fresh parsley, for garnish

recipe continues

Combine the water and saffron in a small bowl and let it infuse for a few minutes. Meanwhile, rinse the rice under cold water until it runs clear. Set aside. Inspect the mussels and discard any with broken shells or that do not close when tapped. Set aside.

Heat 3 tablespoons of the oil in a 12-inch paella pan, skillet, or oven-proof casserole over medium-high heat. Cook the chicken thighs, turning frequently, for 5 minutes, or until crisp and golden. Transfer to a large bowl. Add the chorizo to the pan and cook, stirring, for 1 minute, or until beginning to crisp. Transfer to the bowl with the chicken.

Heat the remaining 3 tablespoons oil in the pan and cook the onions, stirring frequently, for 2 minutes, then add the garlic and paprika and cook, stirring, for another 3 minutes, or until the onions are soft but not browned. Add the rice and green beans, stirring to coat with oil. Return the chicken, chorizo, and any accumulated juices to the pan. Stir in the stock, saffron plus soaking liquid, and salt and pepper to taste. Bring to a boil, stirring constantly. Reduce the heat to low and simmer, uncovered and without stirring, for 15 minutes, or until the rice is almost tender and most of the liquid has been absorbed.

Arrange the mussels, shrimp, and bell pepper evenly on top, then cover the pan and simmer, without stirring, for an additional 5 minutes, or until the shrimp turn pink and the mussels open. Discard any mussels that remain closed.

Taste and adjust the seasoning if necessary. Sprinkle with the parsley and serve immediately.

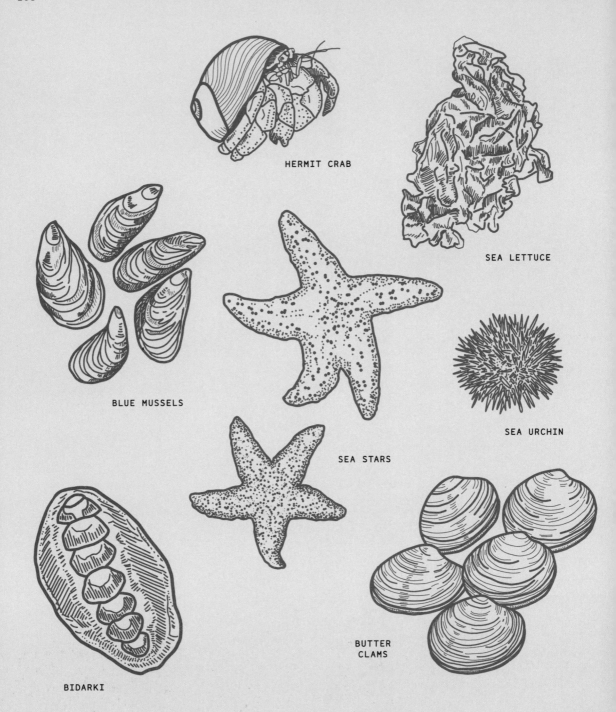

HERMIT CRAB

SEA LETTUCE

BLUE MUSSELS

SEA STARS

SEA URCHIN

BIDARKI

BUTTER
CLAMS

Tide-Pooling and Low-Tide Harvesting

When we were young, our mom used to wake us up early when the tide was low. We rolled out of our bunk beds to pull on our boots, grab butter knives from the kitchen and buckets from the greenhouse, and run toward the beach. Over slippery ribbons of kelp, we made our way toward Stonewall Reef, stopping to peer into tide pools alive with the colorful homes of hermit crabs, anemones, and sea stars. We investigated the homes of tiny invertebrates and watched small fish swim in the puddles left behind by the receding tide.

An amazing array of marine animals live within the intertidal zone between the water's edge and the high tide line, some edible and delicious. We filled our buckets with butter clams and blue mussels to carry home for chowder. We ate sea lettuce—a delicate emerald green seaweed with a salty crunch—straight from the shore. Sea urchins nestled between large rocks and we split them with our butter knives to eat the rich uni inside. *Bidarkis*, a delicacy and important subsistence food source to people of the Aleutian Islands, were one of our favorite low-tide treasures. These black chitons suction to the bottom of rocks with their long orange foot, and are a salty, chewy snack. Octopus lived under the rocks on Stonewall Reef too, identifiable by the small piles of bones and shells left outside their watery caves and occasionally a beautiful red-orange tentacle curled lazily in the kelp. We loved to watch their long tentacles change colors and feel their suctions stick to our fingertips. A few times a year we brought an octopus home with us and enjoyed its tough, chewy succulence in a salad or fried into patties with celery, onions, bread crumbs, and spices.

Tide-pooling is a great way to learn about marine animals in your area. It's surprising how many beautiful colors, graceful movements, and interesting interactions you will witness by simply wandering down to the beach at low tide. To find a good tide pool, look for rocky beaches with large boulders small animals could live beneath, and areas where water collects in pools once the tide goes out. These places provide the best protection for invertebrates and small fish. If you want to identify the creature you find, bring an illustrated field guide and a magnifying glass to examine the marine life closely. Make sure you check a tide table before you go to hit the beach at the right time; you can pick up a tide book at most sporting goods stores.

Before you go, brush up on tide-pooling etiquette:

- Step on bare rock whenever possible, rather than on living organisms like barnacles or periwinkles.

- Turn over small rocks gently and avoid moving large ones. A quick turnover could crush species alongside the rock or those attempting to hide as their home is uncovered.

- Wet your hands with seawater before touching or holding anything living in a tidepool.

- Always replace rocks and seaweed for cover once you finish exploring, and do so carefully.

- Note that you need a permit to remove any sea life from the beach. If you would like to harvest seaweed or shellfish such as clams, crabs, snails, chitons, or octopus, you are required to obtain a license from your state.

Prince William Prawn Summer Rolls

Some summers we fish in Prince William Sound. One of our family's boats is a purse seiner, fishing for pink salmon, and the other is a tender, which brings the salmon delivered by the fleet each night into town to be processed. On the tender, most of the work happens during the evening and late into the night when fishing boats pull up one at a time to off-load the day's catch. The tender crew helps service the boats with fuel, fresh water, and groceries, and then drives to town to off-load at a processing facility. The tender returns to the fishing grounds in the morning and has some downtime before the deliveries start again. This is shrimping time!

Prince William Sound is known for its huge, sweet, delicious spot prawns, and we set pots baited with seafood-flavored canned cat food, herring oil, or a salmon head. We love to boil our catch in Cajun seasoning with corn on the cob, quartered potatoes, and whole garlic cloves. We also love to make Prince William Prawn Summer Rolls because we're often craving the crunch of fresh ingredients at sea. Serve with lots of fresh mint and cilantro, dipped in peanut sauce.

MAKES 16 ROLLS, OR 8 SERVINGS

- 16 raw shell-on prawns or shrimp
- 6 ounces thin rice noodles
- 2 heads butter lettuce, leaves separated, rinsed, and patted dry
- 3 carrots, peeled and cut into 4-inch matchsticks
- 1 red bell pepper, cut into 4-inch matchsticks
- 4 green onions (white and 3 inches of green parts), cut into 4-inch matchsticks
- 16 (8½-inch) rice paper spring roll wrappers
- 32 fresh mint leaves
- 32 small sprigs cilantro
- 1 cup Peanut Dipping Sauce (recipe follows)

recipe continues

Blanch the prawns in a pot of boiling water for 1 to 2 minutes, or until pink and opaque. Remove immediately, dunk into ice water to stop cooking, drain, and cool in the refrigerator. Once cool, remove the shells and halve each prawn lengthwise.

Bring a pot of water to a boil. Add the rice noodles and cook until tender but not mushy, about 6 minutes. Drain and cool under cold running water. Refrigerate until ready to use.

Remove any tough veins from the center of the lettuce leaves and discard. Place the carrots, bell pepper, and green onions in individual bowls.

In a large bowl of cold water, dip a rice paper for about 10 seconds; gently shake off excess water and lay the paper flat on a clean damp kitchen towel. Stack several lettuce leaves on the lower third of the rice paper. Top with 2 to 3 tablespoons of noodles, 2 prawn halves, a few carrots, bell peppers, and green onions, and finally 2 mint leaves and 2 cilantro sprigs.

Fold the bottom edge of the rice paper up over the filling. Fold in the sides, then roll up into a tight cylinder (like a burrito) to seal.

Repeat the assembly process with the remaining ingredients. Store the rolls seam side down and arrange on a serving platter with the dipping sauce. Serve immediately, or if you prefer to prepare the rolls in advance, cover them with a damp kitchen towel for up to 3 hours.

PEANUT DIPPING SAUCE

The perfect complement to Prince William Prawn Summer Rolls, this dipping sauce is so tasty you'll be eating it with a spoon. It's equally delicious over rice bowls, noodles, stir-fried vegetables, and fish.

MAKES ABOUT 1 CUP

- ½ cup hoisin sauce
- ¼ cup smooth peanut butter
- ¼ cup water
- 1 tablespoon rice vinegar
- 1 clove garlic, grated
- 1 teaspoon grated fresh ginger
- 1 tablespoon chopped peanuts, for garnish

Combine all the ingredients except for peanuts in a medium bowl, whisking until well combined. Add more water for a thinner consistency. Transfer the sauce to a small serving bowl and sprinkle with the peanuts. Refrigerate any leftover sauce in an airtight container for up to three days.

Octopus Patties

This recipe is from Anna Hoblet from False Pass, Alaska—whose family has subsisted off the land and sea of the Aleutian Islands for many generations. In western Alaska, octopus are traditionally harvested at low tide and cooked into tender patties, crispy like crab cakes but a little bouncier on your tongue.

MAKES 4 TO 6 SERVINGS

- 2 tablespoons unsalted butter
- ½ cup chopped yellow onion
- 4 large eggs
- ½ cup whole milk
- ½ cup all-purpose flour
- 1 teaspoon baking powder
- 1 teaspoon kosher salt
- ¼ teaspoon freshly ground black pepper
- 3 or 4 octopus legs, boiled and processed in a meat grinder to make 4 cups ground
- Vegetable or peanut oil, for frying

Heat the butter in a large cast-iron pan over medium heat. Sauté the onion until translucent, and set aside. Wipe out pan.

Beat the eggs in a medium mixing bowl. Add the milk and stir to combine.

In a large mixing bowl, stir together the flour, baking powder, salt, and pepper. Add the octopus and sautéed onions, and stir to combine. Add the egg mixture to flour mixture and stir to combine into a resulting mixture that is moist and slightly sticky.

Heat cast-iron pan and add ½ inch oil. Form ½ cup scoops of the octopus mixture into burger-shaped patties. Using a slotted spatula with a long handle, carefully lower the patties into the hot oil. Fry the patties, flipping them once, until both sides of the patties are golden brown, about 3 minutes each side. Serve immediately, and enjoy with your favorite dipping sauce and a side of fresh greens (we like the Crunchy Green Cabbage Salad on page 143).

Tangy Octopus Salad

Octopus patties and octopus salad are two common ways to eat a fresh octopus in western Alaska. The beauty of this tangy, spicy salad is that the simple ingredients could be found at the village store and, aside from the octopus, are most likely already in your refrigerator. It's perfect on its own or eaten with tortilla chips, crackers, or tiny toasts like ceviche. The salad is also great on top of a rice bowl.

MAKES 6 SERVINGS

- 3 octopus legs
- 1 cup chopped celery
- ½ cup chopped carrot
- ½ cup chopped red onion
- 1 jalapeño, chopped
- ½ cup chunky salsa
- ½ cup ketchup
- ½ cup mayonnaise
- ¼ cup Worcestershire sauce
- 3 tablespoons hot sauce, such as Tabasco

Place the octopus in a large pot over medium heat with enough water to cover. Bring the water to a gentle simmer and cook for 1 hour, or until tender. Remove from the pot and let cool.

Chop the octopus into small ¼-inch pieces and add to a large serving bowl. Stir in all the remaining ingredients until well combined. Let the salad chill in the refrigerator for at least 30 minutes before serving. The salad will keep well covered in the refrigerator for up to 3 days.

BIRDS OF ALASKA

PACIFIC GOLDEN-PLOVER

COMMON MURRE

COMMON LOON

RED-FACED CORMORANT

HORNED PUFFIN

GLAUCOUS-WINGED GULL

ARCTIC TERN

BELTED KINGFISHER

BLACK-FOOTED ALBATROSS

RHINOCEROS AUKLET

WESTERN SANDPIPER

BLACK OYSTERCATCHER

Observing the Natural World from the Deck of a Boat

We spend our summers looking out to land from sea. It's an amazing perspective to behold. Seals, sea lions, and otters bask on sunny rocks in the breaking waves. A fox runs down the beach with her kits; a mother brown bear and her cubs trundle through the alders, looking for blueberries. Sometimes, when fishing close to the beach, we might see a wolf or a walrus watching us. We catch glimpses of caves and beautiful rock formations while passing cliffs where seabirds nest. Rising out of the water, rolling hills where caribou roam turn into mountains and above it all, smoking volcanoes. We keep binoculars in the wheelhouse to peer at whale tails on the horizon or an eagle diving to catch a fish. We also keep a paddleboard or kayak on the boat so when we have downtime we can explore the shoreline. We wander the beach in search of pieces of blue and green beach glass, Japanese fishing floats washed into the high tide line, and wild lupines to pick before paddling back out to the boat.

Oysters on the Half Shell

When we fish for salmon in Prince William Sound, we dream all summer that there will be a day when fishing closes and we anchor near Perry Island, where there is a remote oyster farm that delivers oysters to fishing boats that call to shore on the radio.

Once, when the stars aligned, the oyster farmers threw us a few sacks of their freshest and we spent the evening shucking oysters on the back deck, eating them straight from the sea and saving the biggest ones to broil with butter, garlic, and a little parsley.

Though we often use a trusty flathead screwdriver to shuck oysters when we're at sea, it's wise to use an oyster knife, towel, and pair of heavy-duty gloves when shucking at home.

MAKES 4 SERVINGS (3 OYSTERS EACH)

- 1 dozen unshucked oysters

- 1 cup Cilantro Mignonette (recipe follows)

Rinse the oysters well. Put on heavy gloves, then place a clean kitchen towel in your left palm. In the towel, hold the cupped bottom of the shell, with the hinge end facing your wrist.

With your right hand, insert the point of the shucking knife into the hinge end, pressing gently on the hinge until you feel it pop open.

Wipe the knife clean on the towel. With the oyster shell just partway open, slip the knife blade inside. Carefully slide the knife along the underside of the top shell to cut the oyster muscle free. Discard the top shell.

Wipe the knife clean again, then carefully cut the muscle from the bottom shell, reserving as much of the oyster's brine as possible.

Remove any shell pieces that may be floating in the brine and serve immediately on a big platter of ice with the cilantro mignonette.

recipe continues

CILANTRO MIGNONETTE

We love eating oysters straight from the cold saltwater; they are simply perfect as they are. We also love pairing them with this herby mignonette that complements the oyster's briny flavor.

ABOUT 1 CUP

- ⅓ cup rice vinegar
- ⅓ cup seasoned rice vinegar
- Juice from 1 lime (about 2 tablespoons)
- ½ bunch cilantro, chopped
- 1 shallot, chopped

Mix all the ingredients together in a shallow bowl. Using a tiny spoon, serve over freshly shucked oysters.

Oyster Dressing

This recipe, passed down from our Great-Aunt Martha, is a quintessential Midwest side dish turned seafood-focused alternative to traditional stuffing on Thanksgiving. It's the dish that brings people back for seconds and thirds, and we find ourselves scraping the pan clean with our dessert forks as we do the dishes. It's a special dressing to add to your family's holiday spread if you love oysters.

MAKES 8 SERVINGS

- 1 pint oysters, freshly shucked or jarred
- 2 cups saltine cracker crumbs
- ½ cup (1 stick) unsalted butter, melted
- ¾ cup heavy cream
- ¼ cup fresh or jarred oyster liquid
- ½ teaspoon kosher salt
- ¼ teaspoon freshly ground black pepper
- ¼ teaspoon Worcestershire sauce

Preheat the oven to 350 degrees F and butter an 8-inch casserole dish.

Drain the oysters, reserving their liquid. In a medium bowl, mix together the cracker crumbs and melted butter until moistened.

In the casserole, spread a layer of crumb mixture, then one of oysters, another of crumbs, then oysters, and finally top with the remaining crumb mixture.

In a small bowl, whisk together the cream, oyster liquid, salt, pepper, and Worcestershire. Pour evenly over the crumb topping.

Bake the dressing for 40 minutes, until golden. Let cool for 10 minutes, then serve hot with a big serving spoon. Cover any leftovers and store in the refrigerator for up to 5 days.

From the Stonewall Kitchen

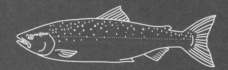

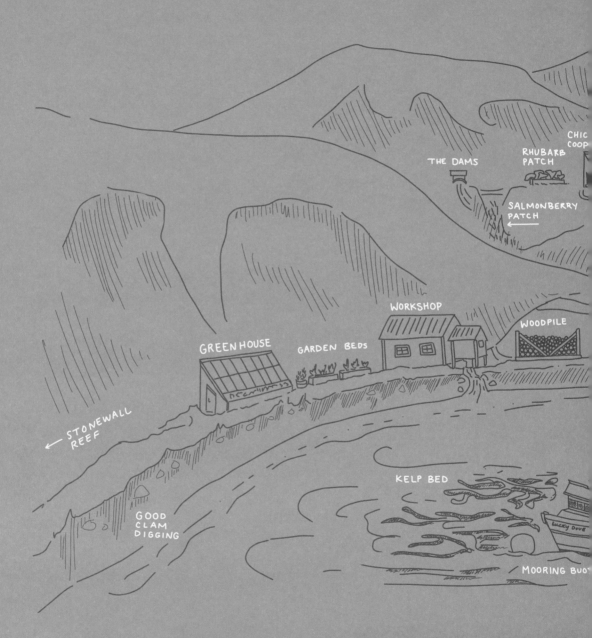

STONEWALL PLA

THE DAMS

RHUBARB PATCH

CHIC COOP

SALMONBERRY PATCH

WORKSHOP

WOODPILE

GREENHOUSE

GARDEN BEDS

STONEWALL REEF

KELP BED

LUCKY DOVE

GOOD CLAM DIGGING

MOORING BUOY

Stonewall Place

Fishing boats traveling west out the Aleutian chain toward the Bering Sea remember passing an unexpected site among smoking volcanoes, treeless hills, and wild whirlpools. Two girls waving from the beach against a backdrop of outbuildings with sauna chimney smoking, fishing net set, garden beds and greenhouse, a trail leading from the beach to a main house on the hill. Fishermen hundreds of miles from home wondered about this fish camp tucked between two reefs in a narrow pass between Alaska's mainland and Unimak Island, surprised that a home could be found in a place so remote, with weather so wild.

A radio call from a captain's wheelhouse to "Stonewall Place" reached our family's living room there. The homestead acted as a waypoint, a lighthouse for boats passing by, a glimpse of human life in a place otherwise far from it.

Stonewall Place is the homestead our parents bought when they moved to Alaska in the years before we were born. The original owners were Ellen Rockwell, who worked as a nurse at Peter Pan Seafoods in False Pass, the village nearby, and Chuck Martinson, who worked as the cannery's radio operator while running the stockroom. He reported the weather forecast to the fishing fleet, gave the general fishing announcements, and coordinated with tenders bringing fish from the boats back to the cannery. Chuck and Ellen lived at Stonewall Place for over a dozen years and spent their winters there much as we did— reading, keeping the woodstove stoked, tinkering in the workshop, and cooking from scratch. The Stonewall kitchen came stocked with Ellen's cookbooks. Most pages in these books had her careful notes in the margins for substitutions and alterations to make the recipes work with the ingredients they had on hand. Chuck's ornate calligraphy labeled rows of glass spice jars on the shelf—from saffron to mustard seed, cloves to tarragon.

Chuck and Ellen's food system was based on simplicity, self-sufficiency, and also necessity. They ordered bulk food from catalogs to reduce packaging and waste, as they had to burn their

trash or take it in their small boat to the village landfill. They made all their food from scratch, as groceries were also a boat ride away, and they pickled and jarred many of their garden vegetables since there was no freezer or refrigerator at the homestead. Our parents had to learn many of these methods for growing, eating, and preserving food themselves when they moved to the homestead, and they have become integral to the way we still eat and live today.

The homestead was originally a trapper's cabin, which Chuck and Ellen built into a small camp run on hydroelectricity from mountain streams and a water wheel, with a main house, wood workshop, and greenhouse. When our family moved in, we maintained and repaired the existing buildings and hydroelectric system, and also added a chicken coop, wood-burning hot tub and sauna, salmon smokehouse, and stone-foundation outhouse. We lived at Stonewall Place year-round through harsh winters and magnificently abundant summers. Our childhood was rich and remarkable, though its reality was challengingly remote as well as extremely dependent on the seasons and the bounty of the land and sea.

We were homeschooled because it was too challenging to get across to the small village school in our skiff during the winter weather. Large floating ice chunks clogged the ocean passage between the tip of the mainland where we lived and Unimak Island, where the village of False Pass and the school were. Bering Sea storms with strong winds and angry waves kept us on our side of the pass, reading books at our kitchen table. Though learning at home meant drawing, creative writing, net mending, knot tying, gardening, and studying ecology, biology, botany, history, mythology, and astrology with our

parents, we loved going to school in the village. There were other kids to play with, new books to read, and a big, bright, warm gym to run around in. A rotating cast of teachers who came from the outside usually stayed a winter or two, running the K-12 classroom and teaching all kids within it. In a typical year, there were between eight and fifteen students.

Aside from our homeschool lessons and our time spent exploring outside, our childhood at Stonewall Place revolved around the procurement, preparation, and preservation of food. Our grandparents in Seattle loaded a pallet twice a year with dry goods and a few treats they knew we'd never otherwise experience, like a pineapple or bananas, not guaranteed to survive the two-week journey on a freighter ship. Otherwise we found a limited supply of canned foods, boxed milk, and frozen meat at the cannery store in False Pass. The rest of what we ate, we grew or caught ourselves.

We mail-ordered seeds from catalogs, and chickens too. The chicks came in a cardboard box to the village post office. The postmaster would call across to our living room on the VHF radio to let us know that a cheeping package had arrived, and if the weather was nice enough to get across in our skiff, we'd take a trip to town. The chickens provided fresh eggs as they matured, and when they stopped laying, became soup and stock and meat for winter. We named our chickens, Guinevere and Columbia, after songs we'd heard or stories we'd read, but we learned to let go of our attachment after a traumatic morning when a brown bear got into the coop.

The village locals taught us about the wealth of the natural landscape. We hiked the tundra hills above the house, always on the lookout for brown bears, our eyes trained for boletus mushrooms, mossberries, blueberries, cranberries, fiddleheads, pushki, and sorrel. July and August meant salmonberries, highbush blueberries, and small, sweet strawberries. We wore our rubber boots everywhere and carried five-gallon buckets up the creek beds, picking fat ripe salmonberries to help our mom make jam, pies, and wine.

Fresh fish was the king of our wild foods, demanding the most work and the most reward. We set a subsistence net in front of our house on our running line in the summers and caught all species of salmon, as well as kelp. We often picked salmon from the net in our kayak, or pulled on waders at low tide to walk out and retrieve the fish from it. These we filleted at our outdoor fish-cleaning table, cutting and packing their tender meat into freezer bags, or stripping them to brine in salt and brown sugar for the smokehouse built on top of pilings, above a brown bear's standing reach.

We spent afternoons in the skiff, stopping at beaches nearby to look for cottonwood logs, which gave off the best flavor in the smokehouse barrel stove. Logs were chopped with a chisel and axe, and kept the fire stoked throughout the day and night. After a few days of wind and smoke, the salmon strips hanging in the smokehouse rafter could be carried down the steep ladder, cut into small pieces, packed into canning jars in our kitchen, and loaded into our mom's pressure cooker. These jars of smoked salmon fed us through the winter.

The Stonewall kitchen was always alive with preparation. Giant bowls of bread dough rising beneath a kitchen towel above the warm stove, flour sprinkled across the tile countertops, fresh eggs from the chicken coop in a bowl ready to be washed, stalks of rhubarb on the kitchen table, jam jars awaiting labeling by a steady hand. Racks of spices and grains lined the walls; an old ship's porthole window made the perfect cooling spot for hot pies; basil and chive plants sunned themselves on the windowsill; the tea kettle kept itself busy on the stovetop.

Life at Stonewall Place revolved around these food rituals-gathering, preparing, and enjoying the surrounding homegrown and wild ingredients. On special evenings we were visited by fishermen friends, who anchored up in front of our homestead and joined us on our large porch on the hill overlooking the ocean. They brought from their boat a fresh salmon to grill, and we made fresh salads overflowing with nasturtiums and geranium petals, warm whole wheat bread, pesto-lemon pasta, and rhubarb custard pie. Fishing stories on the evening air ebbed and flowed into quiet moments reprieved from the drone of the boat's loud diesel engine and into the nurturing hillsides of the Aleutian Islands.

GETTING TO STONEWALL PLACE

Stonewall Place is located 650 miles southwest of Anchorage, out the Aleutian chain. By air, the journey took two flights—the first was two and a half hours from Anchorage to Cold Bay, which holds the record for most overcast town in America, making it quite difficult to fly in and out of. We always factored at least a day to be weathered in. The second leg was a bumpy twenty-minute flight in a tiny four-seat bush plane to the gravel False Pass airstrip, where mail was flown in three times a week. If the weather was nice enough to get across the pass from the village, the last leg was a twenty-minute skiff ride from the dock to our beach.

The other way to travel to Stonewall is by ferry. Since we were kids, the trusty M/V *Tustumena* has run the three days from Homer to False Pass once a month, bringing supplies and people to the Aleutian Islands. The ferry stops in many small villages along the way and continues on to Akutan and Dutch Harbor before it turns around. From the ferry dock in False Pass, we could take our skiff the short journey to Stonewall Place.

BERING S

ATTU

KISKA

ALEUTIAN ISL

ADAK

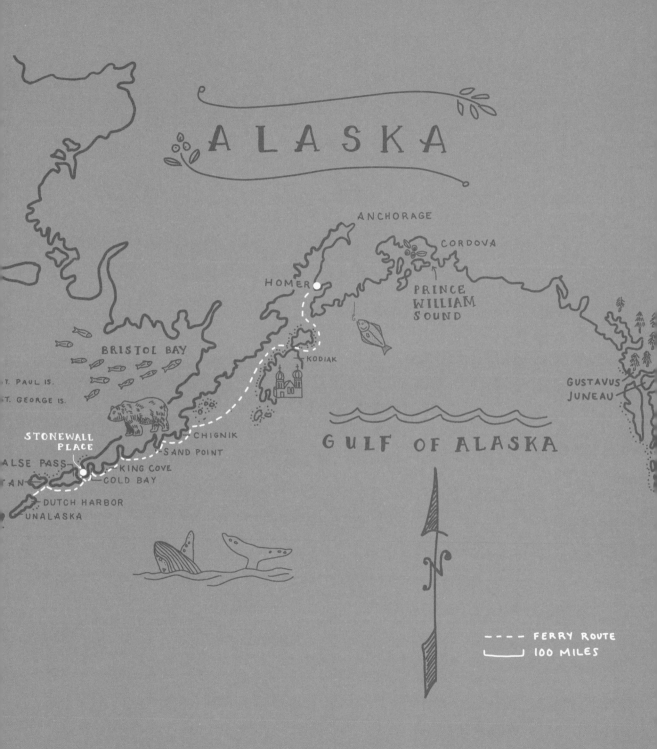

Creamy Carrot Soup

Carrots were one of the first vegetables to sprout in our outside garden beds each summer, and we delighted in those that grew two or three legs braided together or came out of the earth in a rainbow of oranges, yellows, and purples. This creamy carrot soup with cumin, ginger, and fresh chives is a lunchtime favorite around our table during carrot season. You'll need a blender (an immersion blender works best) to puree the soup into hearty, belly-warming bowls, ideally served with a fresh loaf of homemade bread—try Bill's Brainpower Bread (page 178)—slathered with butter.

MAKES 6 TO 8 SERVINGS

- ½ cup (1 stick) unsalted butter
- ½ cup chopped yellow onion
- ½ cup chopped celery
- 10 medium carrots, sliced
- 2 cups chicken stock
- 2 teaspoons cumin
- 1 teaspoon ground ginger
- ½ teaspoon ground white pepper
- 2 cups heavy cream
- Kosher salt
- Chopped fresh chives or green onions, for garnish
- Toasted pepitas, for garnish

Melt the butter in a large saucepan over medium heat. Add the onion and celery; cook until tender, about 5 minutes. Add the carrots, chicken stock, and enough water to cover; bring to boil. Stir in the cumin, ginger, and white pepper, then reduce to a simmer, cover, and cook until the carrots are tender, about 15 minutes.

Transfer the soup in batches to a blender, or use an immersion blender, and puree. Return the soup to the pan, reheating as needed, and stir in the cream. Season to taste with salt. Ladle into soup bowls and sprinkle with fresh chives and pepitas.

Crunchy Green Cabbage Salad

Passed down from our Grandma Diney, this addictively crunchy cabbage salad is one of our favorite dishes to bring to a potluck. The secret ingredient is unexpected—Top Ramen. The noodles are broken up and crisped in butter with sesame seeds and almonds and then tossed into a bed of crunchy green cabbage with a sweet and tangy soy sauce dressing. It's the queen of crowd-pleasing party dishes, and also pairs perfectly with Crispy Beer-Battered Halibut (page 82).

MAKES 6 TO 8 SERVINGS

- 1 stick plus 3 tablespoons unsalted butter
- 4 ounces sliced raw almonds
- ½ cup sesame seeds
- 2 (3-ounce) packages Chicken Flavor Top Ramen
- ½ cup sugar
- ¼ cup rice vinegar
- 2 tablespoons soy sauce
- ¾ cup olive or vegetable oil
- 1 whole head green or napa cabbage, cored and finely chopped
- ½ white onion, finely chopped
- ⅓ cup sliced green onions

Melt the butter in a large sauté pan over medium heat. Add the almonds and sesame seeds. Put the Top Ramen noodles in a large ziplock bag (reserve the seasoning packets). Seal the bag and crush the noodles with a rolling pin or can on the countertop. Add the noodles to the pan, stirring occasionally until golden brown. Remove from the heat and set aside to cool.

In a small saucepan over medium-high heat, whisk the sugar, vinegar, soy sauce, and Top Ramen seasoning packets. Bring to a boil, then remove from the heat and stir in the oil. Transfer to a glass jar and refrigerate until cool.

Mix together the cabbage and white onion in a large salad bowl. Toss the cooled dressing with the cabbage until well coated. Sprinkle with the crunchy topping and green onions, mix lightly, and serve immediately.

French Onion Soup

We always loved our mom's French onion soup as kids—mostly because of the molten cheese on top. It amazes us that a soup this complex and flavorful emerges from a single powerful ingredient. Onions were a vegetable that we could buy at the village store and would keep well in our root cellar at Stonewall Place. Serve this soup in oven-warmed ramekins on a chilly day and feel it heat you from the inside out.

MAKES 6 SERVINGS

- ½ cup (1 stick) unsalted butter
- 2 pounds yellow onions, thinly sliced
- 6 cups beef stock, preferably homemade
- 2 tablespoons Worcestershire sauce
- 1 teaspoon kosher salt
- 1 teaspoon freshly ground black pepper
- ½ teaspoon red pepper flakes
- 6 slices bread, toasted
- 6 slices Gruyère cheese

In a large stockpot over medium heat, melt the butter, then sauté the onions until medium brown, about 4 minutes. Add the beef stock, Worcestershire, salt, and peppers. Bring to a boil, cover, and simmer for 20 minutes.

Preheat the oven to 500 degrees F.

Place a piece of toasted bread into six ovenproof bowls. Ladle soup into each bowl and top with a slice of cheese. Place the bowls on a baking sheet and transfer to the oven until the cheese is bubbly. Serve immediately.

Apricot-and-Honey-Glazed Carrots

Our summertime crop at Stonewall Place was always abundant with hearty root vegetables. Fertilized with kelp and manure from our chicken coop, luscious and leafy carrots with a sweet and delicious crunch grew in the salty sea air. This recipe makes candy-like carrots with a little butter, apricot preserves, and honey.

MAKES 4 SERVINGS

- 1 pound carrots, julienned
- 2 tablespoons unsalted butter
- 2 tablespoons apricot preserves
- 2 teaspoons honey

Cook the carrots in 1 inch of water in a covered medium saucepan until tender, 7 to 8 minutes. Drain.

Meanwhile, in a small saucepan, melt the butter, apricot preserves, and honey, stirring occasionally. Pour the glaze over the carrots and serve immediately.

Village Potlucks

In the village of False Pass near our homestead, whenever anything important happened, there was a potluck. Families gathered together in the school gym to celebrate a graduation, a holiday, an important guest visiting town, a birthday, or the passing of an elder's life. Every family brought a dish that they were known for—whether it was cake, caribou, or canned vegetables. There was always fry bread—deep-fried dough rolled in cinnamon and sugar—and ambrosia salad, decadent with whipped topping, fruit cocktail, and Jell-O. Savory salmon pies, blueberry pies, crowberry pies, and our mom's rhubarb custard pie covered the tables. Some people brought a bucket filled with sea urchins and chitons, called *bidarkis* in Aleut, harvested from the rocks at low tide. The village mayor, Borge, and his wife, Lolly, made chop suey with cans of water chestnuts and baby corn. Gilda made dense, moist, delicious carrot cake. Dol brought her famous pickled fish. Stanley cooked cod tongues and pork scraps. Per brought dried halibut jerky. Ruth brought her king crab pasta salad.

In Alaska, potlucks are a tradition enjoyed most commonly in the winter months. Fishermen have returned home from a long summer season with fish to fill their family's freezers. Many people bring home game from the fall hunting season, or trade fish for wild bird, moose, or caribou meat. Those who stay on land during the summer have been busy smoking, drying, and canning fish; foraging for wild plants and berries; and preserving vegetables from their abundant gardens. Once pantries are stocked, friends gather together to share in the summer season's wild bounty throughout the crisp autumn and quiet light of winter. It is perhaps the greatest feeling of wealth that we have ever known, to sit at a table and eat food that has been caught, foraged, or grown by those sitting around it.

Potlucks are a tradition that can be enjoyed by absolutely everyone, no matter where you live or how you procure
your food. They are a special way to spend time with old friends,
and also an opportunity to welcome new ones. Everyone contrib-
utes to the meal, so hosting doesn't take too much work, and
guests arrive with something they're excited to share. The only
thing you need to do is invite people to your table and ask them
to bring their favorite dish. Soon you'll be sharing a meal with
a story behind every bite.

If you're looking for your own perfect potluck dish, try
one of our family's favorites: Salmon Gravlax (page 62), Prince
William Prawn Summer Rolls (page 111), Crunchy Green Cabbage
Salad (page 143), or Cinnamon-Orange Carrot Cake (page 190).

Kale Caesar Salad

with Avocado Dressing and Buttery Garlic Croutons

Here's to hearty salads that nourish your body and make your taste buds tingle! This kale Caesar is full of avocado, garlic, lemon, and Parmesan, with buttery croutons on top. Kale is one of Alaska's most bountiful leafy greens; it grows happily in the long days of summer sunlight and is resilient in the chilly coastal climate, so we grew and ate a lot of it at Stonewall Place. Sometimes we substitute canned smoked herring for the more traditional anchovy used in Caesar dressings—it adds a wonderful smoky flavor. Pair this with barbecued salmon for a fresh and nutritious meal.

MAKES 6 SERVINGS

FOR THE DRESSING:
- 1 ripe avocado
- ½ cup water
- ¼ cup mayonnaise
- 2 tablespoons freshly squeezed lemon juice
- 2 tablespoons smoked herring or anchovy paste
- 2 small cloves garlic
- 1 teaspoon Dijon mustard
- ½ teaspoon kosher salt

FOR THE CROUTONS:
- ½ cup (1 stick) unsalted butter
- 2 cloves garlic, minced
- 2 teaspoons kosher salt
- 1 loaf crusty French bread, left uncovered overnight and cut into 1-inch cubes

FOR THE SALAD:
- 1 bunch kale, stems removed and leaves chopped (5 to 6 cups)
- ½ cup Parmesan cheese and/or ½ cup pepitas, for garnish

recipe continues

Preheat the oven to 375 degrees F.

To make the dressing, first cut the avocado in half and remove the pit and peel. Cut one half into cubes and reserve for the salad. Blend the other half with the water, mayonnaise, lemon juice, herring, garlic, Dijon, and salt. Taste and adjust seasoning as needed.

To make the croutons, in a large frying pan, melt the butter with the garlic and salt. Remove from the heat and add the bread cubes. Toss with a large spoon until the bread is evenly coated.

Spread the bread cubes on a parchment-lined baking sheet. Bake until golden brown, 15 to 20 minutes. Stir once or twice during baking to ensure even toasting.

To assemble the salad, using salad spoons or tongs, toss the kale with the dressing. Add a handful of Parmesan and pepitas and toss again. Top with the reserved avocado and croutons, and serve immediately.

Pickled Beets

This recipe comes from Ellen, the original owner of Stonewall Place. Our mom uses it now to preserve the beautiful root vegetables from her garden in a sweet and zesty brine. We bring jars of pickled beets on the boat when we go fishing, since it's difficult to get fresh vegetables while at sea. The beets will get more flavorful as they age, so let them sit for at least two weeks before eating; they will store for up to a year in a cool, dark place. Eat them straight from the jar, or as a side with salmon cakes or octopus patties.

MAKES 3 PINTS

- 1½ cups white vinegar
- ½ cup water
- 1 cup sugar
- 1 tablespoon pickling spice
- ½ teaspoon kosher salt
- 2½ pounds beets, washed and trimmed
- 1 yellow onion, cut into thick slices

In a medium saucepan, simmer the vinegar, water, sugar, pickling spice, and salt for 5 minutes. Strain and retain the liquid.

In a large stockpot, cover the beets with water and cook until the skins slip off, 25 to 30 minutes. When the beets are cool enough to handle, peel and slice them into rounds.

Layer the onion and beet slices into 3 pint canning jars. Fill with the pickling solution, leaving 1-inch headspace.

Process the jars in a boiling water bath for 30 minutes. Store in a cool, dark place. The pickled beets will be ready to eat in 2 weeks and can be stored unopened for up to 1 year. Alternatively, you can instead let the beets pickle in the refrigerator for 1 to 2 weeks; be sure to eat within 1 month. (These jars will not be shelf-stable.)

Sautéed Purple Potatoes
with Butter and Chives

In June we carried the potatoes that had sprouted eyes in our root cellar during the spring to our outdoor garden beds. Our mom sliced them in half and we helped plant them—each hole in the dirt finished with a whole herring and a handful of kelp for fertilizer. After twenty hours of daily sunlight in the summer, the potatoes grew full with lanky leaves, and finally in early September, we harvested them as a family. Digging potatoes always felt like a big treasure hunt. We raked through the soil to find the red, yellow, and purple roots that had been growing under their soil blanket. The purple potatoes, our favorites, went straight to the kitchen to be cooked and covered in butter and chives. This recipe makes a wonderful side dish to Sautéed Halibut with Lemon-Pesto Butter (page 85).

MAKES 4 SERVINGS

- 4 cups small whole purple potatoes or large ones cut in half
- ½ cup (1 stick) butter
- ¼ cup chopped green onions or chives
- ¼ cup chopped fresh parsley
- 1 teaspoon kosher salt
- ½ teaspoon freshly ground black pepper
- ½ teaspoon minced fresh dill

There is no need to peel the potatoes, just scrub them well. Bring 1 inch of water to a boil in a large saucepan, then add the potatoes. Cover and cook until tender, 18 to 20 minutes. Drain and plunge the potatoes in a large bowl filled with cold water to stop cooking.

Return the saucepan to medium heat and melt the butter in it. Add the potatoes, green onions, parsley, salt, pepper, and dill. Stir gently to coat the potatoes and heat through. Serve immediately.

Whole Beet Borscht

Lunchtime at our house normally means a pot of soup and a fresh loaf of bread. This whole beet borscht—adapted from *Laurel's Kitchen* by Laurel Robertson, Carol Flinders, and Bronwen Godfrey—is delightful not only for its rich purple color but also for its leafy greens.

MAKES 6 TO 8 SERVINGS

- 8 beets with greens
- 2 quarts vegetable stock
- 1 medium Yukon gold potato, diced
- 1 small yellow onion, chopped
- 2 tablespoons extra-virgin olive oil
- 2 tablespoons all-purpose flour
- Juice from 1 lemon (about 3 tablespoons)
- 2 teaspoons light brown sugar
- 2 teaspoons kosher salt
- ⅛ teaspoon freshly ground black pepper
- ½ teaspoon dried dill
- ¼ teaspoon paprika
- Sour cream, for garnish

Wash the beets and greens. Finely chop the greens and set aside. Peel and grate the beets.

Heat the vegetable stock in a large stockpot over medium heat until boiling. Add the beets, potato, and onion and reduce to simmer, cooking until tender, about 20 minutes.

In a small saucepan over low heat, whisk together the oil and flour and cook for 2 minutes. Add 1 cup of the soup stock slowly into the flour mixture and cook, stirring constantly, until it thickens. Transfer the slurry to the pot.

Add the lemon juice, brown sugar, salt, and pepper, and stir to combine. Stir in the beet greens and cook for 5 to 10 more minutes. Season with the dill and paprika. Taste and adjust the seasonings. Serve each bowl with a dollop of sour cream.

Pickled Asparagus

Our family's pantry has always been full of jarred salmon, jam, and pickled vegetables. This is our Grandma Elaine's secret recipe for pickled asparagus. She has been making it since our mom was a little girl, and when she makes the journey to Alaska to visit, she always brings jars of it packed in her suitcase.

MAKES 1 QUART

- 1 cup water
- 1 cup white vinegar
- 2 tablespoons sugar
- 1 teaspoon pickling salt
- ¼ teaspoon freshly ground black pepper

- 10 to 20 asparagus spears (enough to fit snugly in the jar)
- 1 clove garlic, crushed
- 1 tablespoon fresh dill
- 1 teaspoon red pepper flakes

Bring the water, vinegar, sugar, salt, and pepper to a boil in a medium saucepan. Remove from heat and set aside to cool completely.

Meanwhile, blanch the asparagus. Bring a pot of water to a boil and add the asparagus for 3 to 4 minutes before transferring to a large bowl of ice water.

Place the garlic, dill, and red pepper in the bottom of a quart jar. Pack the asparagus into the jar and fill with the cooled brine with 1-inch headspace.

Process the jar in a boiling water bath for 30 minutes. Store in a cool, dark place. The pickled asparagus will be ready to eat in 2 weeks and can be stored unopened in a cool place for up to 4 months. Alternatively, you can instead let the asparagus pickle in the refrigerator for 1 to 2 weeks; be sure to eat within 1 month. (These jars will not be shelf-stable.)

Fiddlehead-Walnut Pesto

To get to the main house at Stonewall Place, we hiked from the beach up a trail built into the hillside. At one bend in the path was a small grove of fiddlehead ferns that grew in the early summer. We picked them when they were tender and young to sauté and toss into a wild plant salad with sorrel and dandelion greens. Sometimes we made them into a wild pesto to dress pasta, spread over a salmon fillet, or eat on toast with a soft-boiled egg. This pesto calls for basil and fiddleheads, walnuts, garlic, olive oil, and cheese—some of the tastiest ingredients in the world. Be sure to research where fiddleheads grow in your area and know how to identify them properly before you go out foraging. It is best not to eat fiddleheads raw, as some varieties have been known to cause illness in large quantities.

MAKES 1½ CUPS

- 2 cups packed fresh basil leaves
- ½ to ¾ cup fiddleheads, washed, steamed, and chopped
- ⅓ cup walnuts, toasted and chopped
- 2 cloves garlic, smashed
- ½ teaspoon lemon juice
- ½ cup extra-virgin olive oil
- ¼ cup grated Pecorino Romano or Parmesan cheese
- Pinch of kosher salt and freshly ground black pepper

In a food processor, pulse the basil, fiddleheads, walnuts, garlic, and lemon juice until coarsely chopped, scraping the sides as needed. With the motor running, add the oil and process until well mixed. Transfer the pesto to a medium bowl and stir in the cheese, salt, and pepper. Serve over hot pasta, or spread on top of a fillet of salmon then bake. The pesto can be stored in the refrigerator for up to 5 days, or freeze in an ice cube tray and store for up to 2 months.

Glacier Bay Granola

Our mom's first job in Alaska was at the Glacier Bay Country Inn. She learned how to make granola chock-full of dried cherries, apples, apricots, sesame seeds, flax, and coconut. Add your own twist with additional dried fruit, seeds, or nuts and adjusting the sweetness to your liking. Enjoy over homemade yogurt, drizzled with honey and a few fresh blueberries in your bowl.

MAKES 16 CUPS

- ½ cup canola oil
- ½ cup light brown sugar
- ½ cup honey
- 2 tablespoons molasses
- 1 tablespoon vanilla extract
- ½ teaspoon kosher salt
- 8 cups rolled oats
- 1 pound nuts, such as pecans, walnuts, or cashews, chopped
- 2 cups unsweetened coconut flakes
- 8 ounces wheat germ
- ¼ cup flax meal or seeds
- 4 ounces dried raisins or cherries
- 4 ounces dried apples, chopped
- 4 ounces dried apricots, chopped
- Sunflower seeds (optional)
- Pumpkin seeds (optional)
- Dried blueberries (optional)
- Cacao nibs (optional)

Preheat the oven to 350 degrees F.

Combine the oil, brown sugar, honey, molasses, vanilla, and salt in a medium saucepan over low heat. Stir until well combined.

In large bowl toss together the oats, nuts, coconut flakes, wheat germ, and flax. Pour the oil mixture over the oats and stir thoroughly.

Spread the mixture out in a thin layer on 2 large baking sheets and bake for 20 to 25 minutes, stirring every 5 to 10 minutes. After the granola has cooled, stir in the dried fruit. Transfer to quart jars and store in a cool place for up to 1 month.

Homemade Honey Yogurt

We grew up making yogurt at home out of necessity, because yogurt wasn't usually available at the village store. This version is simple, tangy, and a tiny bit sweet. Making yogurt regularly at home is economical because you can just use a few spoonfuls of your last batch to start a new one. To start your first batch, use either store-bought plain yogurt with active cultures, or freeze-dried yogurt starter cultures. It takes about a full day for the yogurt to warm, cool, and set, so make a routine of it and always have a fresh batch for your breakfast.

MAKES 5 CUPS

- ¼ gallon (4 cups) any dairy-based milk, including reconstituted powdered milk, skim milk, whole milk, or raw milk
- 2 tablespoons honey
- 2 tablespoons yogurt from a prior batch, store-bought live, active-culture plain yogurt, or freeze-dried yogurt starter culture, divided

Heat the milk and honey in a stainless steel pan over medium heat, stirring occasionally, until it reaches 180 degrees F.

Pour the heated milk into a clean quart-size jar. Cool on the counter or in a cool water bath until the temperature drops to 115 degrees F.

Add 2 tablespoons of the premade or store-bought yogurt into the jar and stir with a metal spoon—just enough to incorporate into the milk.

Place the jar in the oven with only the light on for 7 to 9 hours—
the longer the yogurt incubates, the creamier, thicker, and tang-
ier it will be. The oven light should provide consistent heat around
110 degrees F; Alternatively, use a 60-watt light bulb to incubate the
jar in a non-drafty spot.

Move the jar to the refrigerator until the yogurt is cold and set. As
the yogurt cools it will continue to thicken. If you prefer a thicker
consistency, pour off the liquid whey from the top or strain the yogurt
in cheesecloth.

The yogurt will keep for up to 10 days. Reserve 2 tablespoons in a ster-
ile jar in the refrigerator until needed to make the next batch. If you'd
like to add fruit to your yogurt, do so after it has incubated in the oven
so you don't upset the bacteria's process.

Old-Fashioned Apple Dumplings

This classic dish is the perfect winter weekend breakfast to make before gearing up and getting out for a day in the snow. These dumplings are warm, flaky, appley sweet, and drizzled with a maple–brown sugar sauce that caramelizes right along with them. Apple dumplings are also a great dessert to make your whole house smell like heaven.

MAKES 8 SERVINGS

- 1 homemade or store-bought pie crust
- 8 Granny Smith apples
- ½ cup raisins, divided
- ¼ cup (½ stick) unsalted butter, divided
- ½ cup packed light brown sugar, divided
- ½ cup maple syrup
- ½ cup water

Divide the pie dough into 8 equal portions. With a rolling pin, roll them out into ¼-inch-thick rounds.

Peel, halve, and core the apples. Place 1 tablespoon of the raisins, 1 teaspoon of butter, and 1 teaspoon of the brown sugar in the center of one apple half. Place the other apple half on top to form a whole apple. Repeat with the remaining apples. Wrap each apple in a dough round and place in a 9-by-13-inch glass baking dish.

Combine the maple syrup, water, and remaining butter and brown sugar in a small saucepan over medium heat. Pour the warm sauce over the apples and bake at 400 degrees F for 1 hour, or until the pastry is golden and the apples are tender. Remove from the oven and spoon with any remaining sauce from the baking dish before serving.

Per's Swedish Pancakes

This skinny pancake recipe—a variation on French crepes or Norwegian pancakes—is from Per Johnson: village car mechanic, trophy halibut fisherman, air traffic controller, bed-and-breakfast host, salmonberry wine aficionado, police officer, and dear friend. He wore wooden clogs and red sweatpants, and drove one of his many fixed-up vans to meet the mail planes at the gravel runway—his Airedale "PJ" (Per Junior) always trailing close behind. Per made these pancakes for breakfast on weather days when we couldn't get back to our homestead in the skiff. They remain one of our favorite ways to start the day. If you are feeding a crowd, double or triple the batch and get several pans going to help you cook as fast as the people can eat! Sprinkle the pancakes with sugar, maple syrup, jam, fresh berries, maybe a dollop of home-made yogurt, or rhubarb sauce. Roll them up tight and enjoy.

MAKES 4 SERVINGS

- 2 cups whole milk
- 1½ cups all-purpose flour
- ⅓ cup sugar
- 3 large eggs

- 1 teaspoon vegetable oil
- Salted butter
- Confectioners' sugar, for sprinkling

In a blender or using an electric hand mixer, mix the milk, flour, sugar, eggs, and vegetable oil until the batter is smooth and the consistency of gravy.

Melt the butter in a large cast-iron or nonstick pan over medium heat. Pour ¼ cup batter into the center of the pan, then pick up the pan with a hot pad and swirl until the batter is spread evenly. When it begins to bubble and firm up, carefully flip the pancake with a thin spatula and cook until lightly golden on both sides. Sprinkle with confectioners' sugar and serve immediately.

Cardamom-Date Waffles

Some days during the winter on our homestead, we woke up and the weather was just too stormy to go outside. Wind howled through the hills at eighty miles per hour, snow blew up around the kitchen windows, and tusk-like icicles hung from the roof. On these mornings, we stoked the fire and were happy to call it a Waffle Day. This harvest wheat batter is sweet and spiced with cardamom and dates.

MAKES 4 SERVINGS

- 2 cups whole milk
- ⅓ cup butter, melted
- ⅓ cup maple syrup
- 2 large eggs, separated
- 1¼ cups all-purpose flour
- ¾ cup whole wheat flour
- ½ cup crushed bran flakes cereal

- 1 tablespoon baking powder
- 1 teaspoon kosher salt
- 1 teaspoon ground cardamom
- ¼ teaspoon baking soda
- Pinch of cream of tartar
- 1 tablespoon sugar
- ¾ cup finely chopped dates

Preheat a waffle iron.

Combine the milk, butter, maple syrup, and egg yolks in a large bowl and whisk to blend. In a separate bowl, combine the flours, cereal, baking powder, salt, cardamom, and baking soda. Add to the wet ingredients and whisk until fairly well mixed. Do not worry if a few lumps remain—they will disappear during cooking.

Beat the egg whites and cream of tartar in another bowl until soft peaks form. Add the sugar and beat until the peaks are stiff but not dry. Gently fold a quarter of the whites into the batter, then fold in the remainder along with the dates.

Ladle the batter into the waffle iron and cook until golden brown, about 5 minutes. Serve immediately with butter and maple syrup.

Blueberry-Apple Dutch Baby

We make Dutch babies to celebrate birthday breakfasts (candles add a festive flair) and to rouse the crew from their bunks in the morning. We make them in the summer when the wild blueberries are ripe and in the winter when we have a pantry full of preserves to spread on top. This puffy pancake doubles or triples in size while baking, so make sure you turn the oven light on before you pull it out to let everyone see its true beauty before it settles. This recipe includes blueberries, apples, and a little lemon zest, but other berries or fruits can be substituted—strawberry and nectarine slices taste nice. Sprinkle with confectioners' sugar, maple syrup, jam, or lemon curd just before serving.

MAKES 4 TO 6 SERVINGS

- 1 cup all-purpose flour
- 1 cup whole milk
- 4 large eggs, slightly beaten
- ¼ cup granulated sugar
- ½ teaspoon finely grated lemon zest
- ¼ teaspoon kosher salt
- Pinch of ground nutmeg
- ½ cup (1 stick) unsalted butter
- 1 cup thin apple slices
- 1 cup blueberries
- ¼ cup confectioners' sugar

Preheat the oven to 425 degrees F.

Combine the flour, milk, eggs, sugar, lemon zest, salt, and nutmeg in a blender or large mixing bowl. Stir lightly, leaving the batter a little lumpy.

Melt the butter in 12-inch cast-iron skillet over high heat. When very hot, remove from the heat carefully and arrange the apple slices in the pan. Pour the batter over the apples and scatter blueberries evenly on top. Bake for 15 to 20 minutes, or until puffed and golden brown. Sprinkle with confectioners' sugar and serve immediately.

Homemade Sourdough Starter

Sourdough has a long and storied history among Alaskan locals. Settlers traveling north during the Klondike Gold Rush carried sourdough starter in their backpacks to make bread as they moved between towns since yeast was often hard to come by. Legend has it that Alaskan miners in the 1890s even slept with their starters to keep them from freezing during the cold winter months. Some local sourdough strains are almost a hundred years old, passed down and maintained through multiple generations.

Having access to one of these well-aged starters isn't necessary to bake a good sourdough loaf or batch of pancakes at home, though it's fun to know its history. Making your own is incredibly easy, and it's not difficult to maintain. Share your starter with friends and family to begin your own sourdough legacy.

MAKES 1 SOURDOUGH STARTER

- 3½ cups all-purpose flour
- 2 tablespoons sugar
- 1 packet (or 2 teaspoons) active dry yeast
- 1 teaspoon kosher salt
- 2 cups lukewarm tap water

In a nonmetal mixing bowl with a wooden spoon, stir together the flour, sugar, yeast, and salt. Never allow sourdough starter to come in contact with metal.

Stir in the water slowly, mixing by hand until the batter is well blended; it will resemble a thick paste. Don't worry about lumps as they will dissolve during fermentation.

Cover the bowl with plastic wrap or a dishtowel, and let it sit in a warm place for 3 to 5 days, stirring the mixture three times each day. The starter will rise and fall over the fermentation period. It's ready when it thins, develops a pleasantly sour flavor, and appears bubbly. Store the starter in a large covered crock in the refrigerator until ready to use.

To use the starter, measure out the amount the recipe calls for and let it warm to room temperature before proceeding, about 4 to 5 hours.

To replenish the starter, add a mixture of 3 cups flour, 2 cups water, 2 tablespoons sugar, and 1 teaspoon salt to the jar and stir to blend with the existing starter. Cover and let sit overnight in a warm place to ferment. In the morning, stir again and return to the refrigerator. Add 1 teaspoon sugar each week to keep the starter active if it's not being used regularly.

Winter Caretaker Sourdough Pancakes

Michael and Sally were our winter caretakers at Stonewall Place when our family began traveling to Homer so that we could attend school there. They brought many food items with them to last the winter, including bowhead whale steaks from the North Slope and sourdough starter in a jar. This sourdough remained at Stonewall for many years afterward, fueling our pancakes and baked goods. This recipe requires a sourdough starter (homemade or purchased), and makes perfect pancakes that are light in the center, crispy on the edges, and delicious with homemade berry jam or apple butter. Cook them in bacon grease for more savory flavor. This base recipe with half a cup of melted butter added also makes fine sourdough waffles.

MAKES 20 MEDIUM PANCAKES

THE NIGHT BEFORE SERVING:

- 4 cups all-purpose flour
- 3½ cups warm water
- 2½ tablespoons sourdough starter
- 1 teaspoon sugar

IN THE MORNING:

- ⅓ cup whole milk
- ¼ cup (½ stick) melted unsalted butter, plus more for greasing the pan
- 2 large eggs
- 2 tablespoons sugar
- 1 teaspoon kosher salt
- 1 teaspoon baking soda

recipe continues

The night before cooking, beat the flour, water, starter, and sugar well in a ceramic mixing bowl. Cover with a clean towel and set somewhere warm overnight.

In the morning, remove 2 tablespoons from the bowl and refrigerate for your next batch of pancakes.

Stir together the remaining sourdough mixture, milk, butter, eggs, sugar, salt, and baking soda until combined. The consistency will be thin.

Heat a cast-iron or nonstick pan over medium heat. Melt butter or bacon grease in the pan and ladle in ¼ cup batter. Cook until bubbles form and the pancake turns golden brown, about 1 minute; flip and cook for 1 more minute. The pancake should be light and have buttery crisp edges. Repeat with the remaining batter and serve immediately.

Apple Butter

Apples and oranges were the most common fruits to find their way to the Aleutian Islands. Layered in cardboard boxes, they rode in the belly of barges coming west from Seattle and were sold at the village store. Working through a box of apples was always a creative endeavor in the kitchen. We dehydrated, stewed and baked them into sauces, cakes, muffins and spreads. Apple butter is one of our favorite things to spread on sourdough pancakes, waffles, biscuits or morning toast. It's also great to bake with and to make sauces for ham or ribs.

MAKES 2½ CUPS

- 6 medium apples, peeled, cored, and finely chopped
- 2 cups packed dark brown sugar
- ½ cup apple cider or juice
- 1 tablespoon freshly squeezed lemon juice
- 1½ teaspoons ground cinnamon
- 1 teaspoon ground nutmeg
- ½ teaspoon ground cloves

Put the apples in a large, heavy-bottomed saucepan or Dutch oven. Add the remaining ingredients and bring to a boil over medium heat. Reduce the heat to a simmer and cook until the apples are soft, about 20 minutes.

Use an immersion blender to puree the mixture. Alternatively, transfer to an upright blender to puree, then return to the pot.

Cook over low heat for about 45 minutes, stirring occasionally to prevent splattering, until the apple butter has thickened to the desired consistency.

Cool completely and store in jars in the refrigerator for up to 3 weeks. Apple butter can also be frozen for up to 6 months.

Breakfast Oatmeal Bread

This is the recipe our mom used to learn how to bake bread from scratch when she moved to Alaska. It's suited well for breakfast because it is a little bit sweet and makes excellent toast to pair with berry jam or apple butter.

MAKES 2 LOAVES

- ½ cup light brown sugar
- 2 tablespoons active dry yeast
- ½ cup warm water
- 2 cups very hot water
- 1 cup rolled oats plus 2 tablespoons
- ½ cup whole wheat flour
- 2 tablespoon unsalted butter
- 5 to 5½ cups all-purpose flour, divided
- 1 tablespoon kosher salt

In a medium bowl, dissolve the brown sugar and yeast in the warm water and set aside.

In a large mixing bowl, combine the hot water, oats, whole wheat flour, and butter and mix well. Add 2 cups of the all-purpose flour and beat with a hand mixer or wooden spoon until well blended, about 3 minutes. When the mixture cools to 110 degrees F, stir in the yeast mixture and enough of the remaining flour to make a moderately stiff dough.

Turn the dough out onto a floured surface and knead for about 10 minutes, or until smooth and elastic. Work it into a ball and place in a greased bowl, turning to coat all sides. Cover and let rise in a warm, draft-free place until doubled in size, 1 to 1½ hours.

Preheat the oven to 350 degrees F.

Punch the dough down, then let it rest for 10 minutes. Divide into two equal portions and shape each into a loaf. Sprinkle 2 tablespoons oats into the bottom of two greased loaf pans to make removing the bread easier after baking. Cover and let rise again until doubled in size, at least 1 hour.

Bake the loaves for 35 to 45 minutes, or until golden brown. Remove from the pans and cool completely on a wire rack.

Potato Lefse

Lefse is a traditional, soft Norwegian potato flatbread. Our Great Granny Faye took pride in the family's Norwegian roots and her potato lefse. She made lefse for our family every holiday until her ninety-fifth birthday, and the tradition has continued with her children, grandchildren, and great-grandchildren today. Our cousins like to wrap their whole Thanksgiving dinner—turkey, stuffing, cranberries and all—in the lefse and eat it like a taco. But traditionally, lefse is enjoyed rolled up with butter and a sprinkle of brown sugar. It's as versatile as other flatbreads, with an additional density that sets it apart. Be sure to leave time to start this recipe the night before you intend to enjoy your batch of lefse.

MAKES 20 TO 25 LEFSE

- 6 russet potatoes, peeled
- ¾ cup heavy cream
- 6 tablespoons unsalted butter, at room temperature
- 1½ teaspoon kosher salt
- 3¾ cups all-purpose flour

In a large stockpot over medium-high heat, boil the potatoes until tender. Drain, then let cool. Push the potatoes through a ricer into a large bowl, cover, and refrigerate overnight.

The next day, let the potatoes sit at room temperature for 10 minutes.

Add cream, butter, salt, and flour, and knead on a floured surface for about 3 minutes, until everything is well mixed. Test the consistency of the dough. You are looking for a texture similar to light pie dough—it should form into a ball without sticking to your hands and hold its shape without cracking if you press the lightly with your thumb. If the dough feels too sticky, knead in a little more flour; if it is too dry or is cracking when pressed, add another couple pats of butter. Taste the dough as you test; it should taste like potatoes, not flour, slightly salty, and buttery.

Cover dough loosely and let rest for 10 minutes, then divide into balls about the size of golf balls. Roll out dough on floured surface as thinly as possible to make a round shape about 8 inches in diameter and ⅛ inch thick.

Warm a lefse griddle or large cast-iron pan to 400 degrees F.

Using a lefse stick or thin spatula, transfer the lefse to the griddle. Cook until bubbles form and the underside has browned in spots, then flip and repeat, about 2 minutes per side. Cover the lefse with a slightly damp towel until ready to serve.

Lefse can be made 1 to 2 days ahead and stored tightly wrapped at room temperature.

Bill's Brainpower Bread

Bill came to teach in False Pass when we were in elementary school, and he stayed for several winters. Though he had lived in the small town of Haines for many years in southeast Alaska, False Pass was a place unlike anywhere he had ever been. He tells us that we were his comic relief while he taught there—the girls who showed up at school every few weeks dressed in rain gear and life jackets from the cold boat ride across the pass, ready to learn anything and everything he could teach. This protein-packed seedy whole grain bread recipe, along with his thimbleberry jam and chocolate cheesecake, is the legacy he has left with our family.

MAKES 1 LOAF

- 1 cup lukewarm water
- 2 tablespoon active dry yeast
- ½ cup honey plus 1 teaspoon, divided
- 5 cups all-purpose flour, divided
- 2 cups whole wheat flour
- 2 cups warm water
- 1 cup dry milk
- ⅓ cup vegetable oil
- 1 large egg, beaten
- 4 teaspoons kosher salt
- 1 cup cooked oatmeal
- ½ cup cornmeal
- ½ cup flaxseed meal
- ½ cup wheat germ
- ½ cup walnuts, chopped
- ½ cup sunflower seeds (optional)
- ¼ cup poppy seeds (optional)

In a small bowl, mix the lukewarm water, yeast, and 1 teaspoon of honey.

In a large mixing bowl, stir together 2 cups of the all-purpose flour with the whole wheat flour, warm water, dry milk, and ½ cup honey. Add the yeast mixture and beat well with a big wooden spoon for one hundred strokes. Cover the bowl and let the dough rise for 45 minutes in a warm place.

Stir in the remaining 3 cups all-purpose flour, oil, egg, and salt. Add the oatmeal, cornmeal, flax, and wheat germ and stir to combine. Add the walnuts and seeds. Knead the dough with additional flour as needed. Let rise for 50 to 60 minutes, or until doubled.

Preheat the oven to 350 degrees F.

Punch down the dough and transfer into a greased bread pan. Let rise for 20 to 25 minutes. Bake for 1 hour, or until golden brown. Remove from baking pans and let cool on a wire rack for 20 minutes before serving.

Olga Bay Cardamom Bread

This recipe comes from Nina, a family friend and Kodiak Island salmon fisherman. The influence of Scandinavian food is strong in Alaska and in our family's Norwegian heritage. Cardamom is the star of many baked goods made in our kitchen. Enjoy this braided loaf spread with Wild Cranberry–Orange Butter (page 182).

MAKES 2 LARGE LOAVES

- 2 tablespoons active dry yeast
- 1 cup plus 5 tablespoons sugar, divided
- ½ cup warm water
- 1½ cups (3 sticks) unsalted butter
- 2¼ cups whole milk
- 4 large eggs
- 2 tablespoons ground cardamom
- 1 tablespoon kosher salt
- 9 to 10 cups all-purpose flour
- ⅓ cup unsalted butter, melted

In a small bowl, dissolve the yeast and 1 tablespoon of the sugar in the warm water. Set aside.

Melt the sticks of butter in a small saucepan over medium heat. Add the milk and warm through.

In a large bowl, whisk together the eggs and remaining 1¼ cups sugar until fluffy. Add the milk mixture, yeast mixture, cardamom, and salt. Stir in flour until the mixture is stiff, then transfer dough to floured surface to knead well. Continue to add flour and knead until the dough is firm and not sticky. Return the dough to the bowl, cover, and let rise in a warm place until it has doubled in size, 50 to 60 minutes.

Preheat the oven to 350 degrees F.

Divide the dough into 2 equal parts. Divide each part into 3 equal parts; roll them out into long ropes and braid together. Place both braided loaves on a greased baking sheet and bake for 20 to 25 minutes. Remove the loaves from the oven and brush with the melted butter. Transfer to a rack to cool.

Wild Cranberry–Orange Butter

This is the perfect sweet and tart spread to melt into a piece of fresh, warm Olga Bay Cardamom Bread (page 180).

MAKES ABOUT 2 CUPS

- 1 cup (2 sticks) unsalted butter, softened
- 3 tablespoons honey
- ½ cup wild cranberries, finely chopped
- ⅓ cup walnuts, finely chopped
- Zest from 1 orange
- ½ teaspoon kosher salt
- ½ teaspoon ground cinnamon

In a medium mixing bowl, whip the butter and honey with an electric mixer until light and fluffy. Add the remaining ingredients and mix on medium speed until combined. Store in an airtight container in the refrigerator for up to 1 week or in the freezer for up to 1 month.

Rhubarb Sauce

Rhubarb grows heartily in Alaska. The rhubarb patch behind our house grew back with incredible volume each summer—stalks as thick as broomsticks. We picked rhubarb for pies and sauces like this one, which is delicious on ice cream, pancakes, cakes, or stirred into a bowl of morning yogurt and granola.

MAKES 6 SERVINGS

- 4 cups rhubarb, cut into
  ½-inch pieces
- 1 cup sugar

- ½ cup water
- ½ teaspoon vanilla extract
- Pinch of kosher salt

Combine the rhubarb, sugar, water, vanilla, and salt in heavy-bottomed saucepan over high heat. Bring to a boil, then reduce to medium-low. Cook for 8 to 10 minutes, stirring occasionally.

Remove from the heat and let cool. Store the sauce in an airtight container in the refrigerator for up to 1 week. It can also be frozen for up to 3 months.

Rhubarb Custard Pie

Our mom says she knew her relationship with our dad was getting serious when he bought her a pair of Xtratuf boots, iconic fishermen's footwear in Alaska, and when she made him a rhubarb custard pie. She has continued to make him rhubarb pies every year on his birthday, which falls in late May when the rhubarb patch is in full glory. This pie is decadent with its creamy custard and tangy fruit, a year-round favorite in our house with fresh or frozen rhubarb.

MAKES 8 SERVINGS

FOR THE CRUST:
- 1 cup all-purpose flour
- ½ teaspoon kosher salt
- ⅓ cup shortening
- 3 tablespoons cold water

FOR THE FILLING:
- 5 large stalks fresh rhubarb, cut into ½-inch pieces (4 to 5 cups)
- 2 cups sugar
- 1 cup all-purpose flour
- 5 egg yolks
- ⅓ cup whole milk

To make the crust, in a medium bowl, mix the flour and salt. Cut in the shortening with a pastry blender until the particles resemble small peas. Add the cold water, 1 tablespoon at a time, tossing with a fork until the flour is evenly moistened—1 to 2 teaspoons more water can be added if necessary.

Form the pastry into a ball, then shape it into a flattened round on a lightly floured surface. Wrap in plastic wrap and refrigerate for about 45 minutes, or until the dough is firm yet pliable. This helps make the baked pastry more flaky. If refrigerated for longer, let the pastry soften for a few minutes before rolling out.

Preheat the oven to 450 degrees F.

On a lightly floured surface, roll out the pastry to fit a 9-inch pie pan. Transfer the pastry to the pan, trimming the dough to leave a 1-inch overhang. Fold it gently over the rim, pressing it to the sides and fluting the edges with your fingers.

To make the filling, arrange the rhubarb in the pie shell. In a small bowl, stir together the sugar, flour, egg yolks, and milk, then pour the custard over the rhubarb.

Bake for 10 minutes, then reduce the oven temperature to 350 degrees F and bake for 40 minutes, or until the crust is golden brown and filling is set. Set on a rack to cool completely before serving.

Sourdough Chocolate Cake

Bake like an Alaskan old-timer and enjoy this decadent chocolate cake. It's made with a sourdough base (you'll need starter), but never fear—this cake isn't sour, it's just rich with a delicious chocolate flavor. Best topped with Chocolate-Butterscotch Frosting (recipe follows) and served with ice cream and birthday candles.

MAKES 18 SERVINGS

THE NIGHT BEFORE:
- 1½ cups all-purpose flour
- 1 cup water
- ½ cup sourdough starter
- ¼ cup nonfat powdered milk

IN THE MORNING:
- 1 cup sugar
- ½ cup (1 stick) unsalted butter

- 1½ teaspoons baking soda
- 1 teaspoon vanilla extract
- 1 teaspoon ground cinnamon
- ½ teaspoon kosher salt
- 2 large eggs
- 3 ounces unsweetened baking chocolate, melted
- Chocolate-Butterscotch Frosting (recipe follows)

The night before baking (or at least 2 to 3 hours before starting the cake), mix together the flour, water, starter, and dry milk and set in a warm place. It should turn bubbly and there should be a clean, mild sour odor.

In the morning, preheat the oven to 350 degrees F.

In a stand mixer, cream together the sugar, butter, baking soda, vanilla, cinnamon, and salt. Add the eggs one at a time, beating well with each addition. Add the melted chocolate and sourdough mixture, and stir for 300 strokes or at low speed until blended.

Pour the batter into 2 round cake pans or one 9-by-13-inch pan. Bake for 25 to 30 minutes, or until a toothpick inserted in the cake's center comes out clean.

Allow the cake to cool completely before frosting the sides and top of the cake using a butter knife.

CHOCOLATE-BUTTERSCOTCH FROSTING

This is a perfectly decadent frosting to complement the Sourdough Chocolate Cake.

MAKES FROSTING FOR 1 CAKE (18 SERVINGS)

- ⅔ cup packed light brown sugar
- ½ cup light whipping cream
- ¼ cup (½ stick) unsalted butter
- ¼ teaspoon kosher salt
- 3 ounces unsweetened baking chocolate
- 1 teaspoon vanilla extract
- 3 cups confectioners' sugar, sifted

In a saucepan, combine the brown sugar, cream, butter, chocolate, and salt. Bring to a boil, stirring constantly, until the chocolate is melted.

Remove from the heat and add the vanilla and enough confectioners' sugar, 1 cup at a time, for a good spreading consistency. It may be on the runny side, but the frosting will set up after cooling.

Cinnamon-Orange Carrot Cake

A potluck favorite in False Pass, this deliciously moist carrot cake by Gilda Shellikoff is made with coconut, cinnamon, carrots, and canned mandarin oranges. The ingredients are ones that were always reliably stocked on the village store's shelves—fresh fruit was rare, but canned fruit was plentiful and carrots kept well through the seasons. Boxed cake mixes and canned frosting were also common, but none compared to this homemade carrot cake. Frost with your favorite cream cheese icing.

MAKES 10 SERVINGS

- 3 cups all-purpose flour
- 2 cups sugar
- 2 cups shredded carrots
- 1¼ cups vegetable oil
- 1 cup shredded unsweetened coconut
- 1 (11-ounce) can mandarin orange segments, undrained

- 3 large eggs
- 2½ teaspoons baking soda
- 2 teaspoons vanilla extract
- 1 teaspoon freshly grated orange peel
- 1 teaspoon ground cinnamon
- 1 teaspoon kosher salt

Preheat the oven to 350 degrees F. Oil a 9-by-13-inch pan.

Lightly spoon flour into a measuring cup and level off, adding it to a large mixing bowl with each full cup. Add the remaining ingredients to the bowl, mixing with electric beaters at low speed until moistened, and then beat for 2 minutes at high speed.

Pour the batter into the pan and bake for 45 to 50 minutes, or until a toothpick inserted into the center comes out clean. Cool completely before frosting.

Wild Blueberry Crumble

Wild blueberries grow all over Alaska—in the Aleutians on the hillsides behind our homestead and on many shores where we anchor our fishing boat. We carry berry buckets to the water's edge or hike into ravines to sit in a good berry patch, listen to sparrows sing, and pick until our fingers are stained with berry juice. This crumble is quick, easy, and so tasty still warm from the oven with a scoop of vanilla ice cream.

MAKES 8 SERVINGS

FOR THE FILLING:

- 2 pounds (about 6 cups) fresh blueberries
- ½ to ¾ cup sugar, depending on the tartness of the berries
- 2 tablespoons all-purpose flour
- 1 tablespoon freshly squeezed lemon juice
- ¼ teaspoon kosher salt

FOR THE CRUMBLE:

- 1 cup all-purpose flour
- ½ cup rolled oats
- ½ cup packed light brown sugar
- ½ teaspoon vanilla extract
- ½ teaspoon kosher salt
- ½ cup (1 stick) unsalted butter, cut into cubes

Preheat the oven to 375 degrees F. Grease a 9-inch pie pan.

To make the filling, stir together the blueberries, sugar, flour, lemon juice, and salt. Transfer to the pie pan.

To make the crumble, in a large bowl, stir together the flour, oats, brown sugar, vanilla, and salt. Mix in the butter with your fingertips or a pastry cutter until well combined. Crumble the topping evenly over the berries.

Bake for 30 to 40 minutes, or until the filling is bubbling and the topping is lightly browned. Let the crumble cool for about 30 minutes before serving.

Overnight Caramel-Pecan Rolls

When we're fishing, we like to start these nutty, gooey sweet rolls before we head to our bunks for the night. In the morning we pop them in the oven to bake, and enjoy them with a pot of coffee and a good book in the wheelhouse. They make the whole galley smell delicious, and the crew wakes up with big sleepy smiles on their faces.

MAKES 18 ROLLS

- 3 to 3¼ cups all-purpose flour, divided
- 2¼ teaspoons active dry yeast
- 1 cup plus 2 tablespoons whole milk
- 1½ tablespoons shortening
- 5 tablespoons granulated sugar, divided
- 1 teaspoon kosher salt
- 6 tablespoons unsalted butter, softened, divided
- ½ cup packed brown sugar
- 1 tablespoon light corn syrup
- ½ cup pecan halves
- ½ teaspoon ground cinnamon

Several hours or the night before baking, prep the dough. In a large mixing bowl, stir together 1¼ cups of the flour and the yeast. Heat the milk, shortening, 1 tablespoon of the granulated sugar, and salt in a small saucepan until just warm (120 degrees F) and the shortening is nearly melted, stirring constantly. Add to the flour mixture and beat on low speed for 30 seconds, scraping the sides of the bowl, then beat on high speed for 3 more minutes.

Turn the dough out onto a lightly floured surface and knead in as much of the remaining flour as possible to make a soft dough that is smooth and elastic. Shape into a ball, cover, and let rest for 20 minutes in a warm place.

In a small saucepan over medium heat, melt ¼ cup of the butter, then stir in the brown sugar and corn syrup. Stir just until blended. Distribute the mixture evenly in the bottom of 18 greased muffin cups. Sprinkle the pecans evenly into each cup. Set aside.

With a rolling pin, roll the dough into an 18-by-10-inch rectangle on a lightly floured surface. Spread with the remaining 2 tablespoons butter. Combine the remaining ¼ cup granulated sugar with the cinnamon and sprinkle over the dough. After pressing it in and fluting the edges with your fingers, prick the bottom and sides of the crust with a fork to allow steam to escape while baking. Using a sharp knife, cut the dough into eighteen 1-inch-thick slices. Place the rolls cut side down in the muffin cups. Cover with plastic wrap and chill in the refrigerator for 2 hours.

When you're ready to bake the rolls, preheat the oven to 375 degrees F.

Let the pans sit at room temperature, covered, for 20 minutes. Bake the rolls for 20 minutes, or until lightly golden. Invert onto a wire rack. Serve warm.

Chocolate Chip and Walnut Banana Bread

Bananas were rare in remote Alaska, but on the occasion that they arrived on a barge, they were usually past ripe and speckled with brown spots. The only thing to do was load a box of brown bananas into our skiff, take them home, and make banana bread in the Stonewall kitchen. With gooey chocolate chips and crunchy walnuts, this loaf is most delicious still warm with butter.

MAKES 1 LOAF

- ½ cup (1 stick) unsalted butter
- 1 cup sugar
- 1 cup mashed very ripe bananas (about 2 whole)
- 2 large eggs
- 2 cups all-purpose flour
- 1 teaspoon baking soda
- ½ teaspoon kosher salt
- ⅓ cup whole milk
- 1 teaspoon freshly squeezed lemon juice
- 1 cup chocolate chips
- ½ cup walnuts, chopped

Preheat the oven to 350 degrees F. Grease a 9-by-5-by-3-inch loaf pan and set aside.

In a large mixing bowl, cream the butter and gradually add the sugar. Mix well. Add the bananas and eggs and blend thoroughly.

In a separate bowl, sift the flour with the baking soda and salt. In another bowl, combine the milk and lemon juice (this will cause the milk to sour and curdle). Slowly and alternately, fold the flour mixture and the milk mixture into the butter mixture, beginning and ending with the flour mixture. Blend well after each addition. Stir in the chocolate chips and walnuts.

Pour the batter into the pan and bake for 1 hour, or until the bread springs back when lightly pressed in the center. Let the bread cool in the pan for a few minutes before turning it out onto a rack to cool.

Zucchini Bread

Zucchini is a fun vegetable to have in your garden because it can grow to such amazing sizes and shapes. The challenge is that sometimes your patch of zucchini ripens all at the same time and you end up with more than you know what to do with. Make this quick and tasty breakfast bread with notes of ginger, cinnamon, and cloves.

MAKES 2 LOAVES

- 2 cups packed light brown sugar
- 1 cup vegetable oil
- 3 large eggs
- 1 teaspoon vanilla extract
- 2 cups grated zucchini
- 1 cup chopped walnuts
- 2 cups whole wheat flour
- 1 cup all-purpose flour
- 1¼ teaspoons baking powder
- 1 teaspoon kosher salt
- 1 teaspoon baking soda
- 1 teaspoon ground ginger
- 1 teaspoon ground cinnamon
- 1 teaspoon ground cloves

Preheat the oven to 350 degrees F. Grease and flour two loaf pans or muffin tins.

In a large mixing bowl, beat together the brown sugar, oil, eggs, and vanilla. Stir in the zucchini and walnuts. In a separate bowl, combine the remaining ingredients and whisk to combine. Add to the zucchini batter, stirring until blended.

Spoon the batter into the loaf pans or muffin tins. Bake for 40 minutes for a loaf, or 20 minutes for muffins. Set on a rack to cool completely before slicing.

Lemon Meringue Pie

Lemons are coveted in our kitchen. We use them for everything from fish to pasta to pie—but this recipe makes them sing. Our grandpa loved lemon meringue pie, and we make it in his honor when we're craving a zesty, sweet, and fresh dessert.

MAKES 8 SERVINGS

FOR THE CRUST:

- 1 cup all-purpose flour
- ½ teaspoon kosher salt
- ⅓ cup shortening
- 3 tablespoons cold water

- ½ cup freshly squeezed lemon juice (from about 3 lemons)
- 3 tablespoons unsalted butter
- 2 teaspoons freshly grated lemon zest

FOR THE FILLING:

- 4 egg yolks (reserve the whites for the meringue)
- 1½ cups sugar
- 6 tablespoons cornstarch
- ¼ teaspoon kosher salt
- 1½ cups water

FOR THE MERINGUE TOPPING:

- 4 egg whites
- 1 teaspoon freshly squeezed lemon juice
- ¼ teaspoon cream of tartar
- 5 tablespoons sugar
- ½ teaspoon vanilla extract

To make the crust, in a medium bowl, mix the flour and salt. Cut in the shortening with a pastry blender until the particles resemble small peas. Add the cold water, 1 tablespoon at a time, tossing with a fork until the flour is evenly moistened—1 to 2 teaspoons more water can be added if necessary.

Form the pastry into a ball, then shape it into a flattened round on a lightly floured surface. Wrap in plastic wrap and refrigerate for about 45 minutes, or until the dough is firm yet pliable. This helps make the baked pastry more flaky. If refrigerated for longer, let the pastry soften for a few minutes before rolling out.

recipe continues

Preheat the oven to 450 degrees F.

On a lightly floured surface, roll out the pastry to fit a 9-inch pie pan. Transfer the pastry to the pan, trimming the dough to leave a 1-inch overhang. Fold it gently over the rim, pressing it to the sides and fluting the edges with your fingers. Bake crust for 15 minutes or until light brown. Cool completely.

Reduce the oven temperature to 350 degrees F.

To make the filling, in a medium bowl, beat the egg yolks with a fork or whisk until blended. In a medium saucepan, whisk together the sugar, cornstarch, and salt, then slowly stir in the water. Set the pan over medium heat, stirring constantly, until the mixture thickens. Boil and continue stirring for 1 minute.

Whisk half of the hot mixture into the egg yolks, then stir it back into the saucepan, whisking constantly. Boil and stir for 2 to 3 more minutes, then remove from the heat. Stir in the lemon juice, butter, and lemon zest. Pour the mixture into the pastry crust.

To make the meringue, in another bowl, beat the egg whites, lemon juice, and cream of tartar with an electric mixer on high speed until it becomes foamy and soft. Slowly beat in the sugar, 1 tablespoon at a time, until it turns glossy and holds stiff peaks. Beat in the vanilla. Spread the mixture over the hot filling, carefully covering it completely to prevent shrinkage. Use a spoon to create light peaks in the meringue.

Bake the pie on the center rack for 20 to 25 minutes, or until the meringue is golden. Cool at room temperature for 1 hour. Cover and refrigerate the cooled pie for 4 hours or until filling is set. Pie can be stored in the refrigerator, loosely covered, for up to 5 days.

Acknowledgments

A few summers ago, an exciting email reached us at sea from Gary Luke, publisher at Sasquatch Books. When we returned home after the fishing season, we embarked together on the journey of writing this book. We are filled with gratitude for the opportunity to share the story of Alaska seafood and recipes from our family, and for Sasquatch taking a chance on fishermen and first-time authors. Thank you to the dream team at Sasquatch for making beautiful sense of the words, images, and illustrations we created for this book.

Thanks to our book agent and fairy godmother, Sandra Bishop, who understood the vision from day one and helped us sail smoothly through the publishing process.

We're grateful for Brian Grobleski, a true creative partner whose photographs brought these recipes to life, and Scott Dickerson, Sashwa Burrous, Camrin Dengel, and Dawn Heumann, whose photos and friendship have helped us tell this story.

Our mom and dad are the reason we have a special story to tell and recipes to share. Thank you for raising us in the wild and for always putting family and good food first.

Thanks to all the people of the Aleutian Islands who taught our family how to harvest and eat from the land and sea when we began our life at Stonewall Place.

We can't wait to share this book with our Salmon Sisters community, who has supported our small business and inspired us with their own stories and recipes over the years. This book is *for* you, and also *because* of you.

Index

Note: Page numbers in *italic* refer to photographs.